LACE FOR CHILDREN OF ALL AGES

by Christine Springett

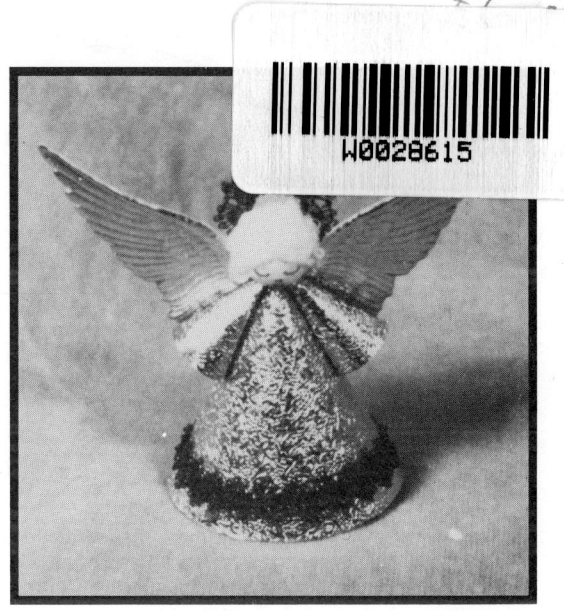

INDEX

Glossary of Terms & Techniques	3

BOOKMARKS

Snake Bookmark	5
Simple Torchon Candle	6
Torchon Candle	8
A Crinoline Lady	10
Simple Flowers	12
Gift Tag & Gift Box	13
Earrings & Small Flower Spray	13
Alice Band	14
Corsage	15

CARDS FOR ALL OCCASIONS

Wedding & Anniversary Cards	16
Birthday Cards	17
Birth Congratulations Card	18
Easter Card	18
Torchon Trim for a Hair Slide or Pony Tail Band	19

HEARTS FOR VALENTINES, WEDDINGS & ANNIVERSARIES

Tiny Tape Lace Heart	21
Large Tape Lace Heart	22
Heart with Raised Chain	23
Double Layer Heart	23
Heart Edging with Heart-Shaped Fan	25

WEDDING HORSESHOES

Wedding or Anniversary Card	27
A Bride's Horseshoe	28

HAIRBANDS

Hairband 1	30
Hairband 2	32
Candle Flounce	34

FRAME EDGINGS

Fine Torchon Edging	38
Simple Leaf Edging	42

CHRISTMAS PROJECTS

Tape Lace Candle	44
Circular Torchon Edging	46
Small Torchon Candle	47
Christmas Flowers	49

HALF STITCH CIRCLES

Smallest Half Stitch Circle	50
Medium Half Stitch Circle	51
Large Half Stitch Circle	51

DECORATED CHRISTMAS BALLS

Simple Cloth Stitch Strip	53
'Kisses'	54
'Chain'	55
'Zig-Zag'	55
'Crosses'	56
'Criss-Cross'	57
'Loop the Loop'	57

CHRISTMAS DECORATIONS IN RINGS

Snowflake, Diamond & Flower	58
Zig-Zag Circles	60
Daisy Rings	62
Sequin Flowers	63
Half Stitch Circle with Sequins	64
Ring with Bell	65
Angels for your Christmas Tree	66
Equipment	72

ACKNOWLEDGEMENTS

My sincere thanks must go to my family who have encouraged me, and nagged me unmercifully, from the start to the finish of this project. My parents have willingly taken over many of my jobs in order to give me time to commit my thoughts to paper. David has once again tackled the difficult task of photographing each item. My sister Ruth has shown great patience with my frequently inept performances on the computer. As time is always in short supply I would like to thank my friend Janet Dutton for working many of the projects so beautifully. It is also thanks to Janet that the flowers on the sprays and many of the cards have been so artistically arranged. I would also like to say a big thankyou to all the children who have made up my weekly class over the past four years. Their enthusiasm and willingness as guinea pigs have made the development of all these projects both possible and enjoyable! I'm grateful to my nephew Steven Crowe for allowing me to use the Mother's Day card he made when aged 7, and to Louise Storer for proving such a talented model.

All of the projects included are completely original although I would point out that the inspiration for my snake bookmark pattern is based on an idea by Chris Berrow and Mellis Eling.

If you have enjoyed this book then look out for "THE CHRISTMAS LACE BOOK" by Christine Springett available April 1991 from C & D Springett, 21 Hillmorton Road, Rugby, Warwickshire, CV22 5DF.

Published by C & D Springett
21 Hillmorton Road,
Rugby,
Warwickshire
CV22 5DF

Printed by Apex Printers
1 Avon Industrial Estate,
Butlers Leap,
Rugby, Warwickshire
CV21 3UT

© C.V. Springett 1989   ISBN 0 9517157 0 4

A GLOSSARY OF TERMS AND TECHNIQUES.

Cloth Stitch. Also known as 'linen' stitch or in the UK as 'whole' stitch. Number the positions of the four bobbins from the left, lift 2 over 3 (also called a 'cross'), now lift the bobbin in position 4 over 3 and 2 over 1 (also called 'twists') and finally lift 2 over 3 to complete the stitch. N.B. It is the POSITIONS not the bobbins themselves which are numbered, and the positions are ALWAYS numbered from left to right.

Collecting Knot. I always use a 'collecting knot' to bring a large number of threads into a tight group. Take the two outside threads, one from each edge, and tie the first part of a reef knot with an extra twist (see below), pull it tight and then, lifting the bunch of centre threads, pass the knotting thread from the left underneath to the right, and the righthand thread underneath to the left. Now tie a reef knot on top, again putting an extra twist on the first half of the knot.

Covering a pin. A pin is 'covered' when a stitch is worked immediately underneath it. In torchon lace the stitch beneath the pin is usually the same as the stitch used above it.

Double Half Stitch. Often used at the end of a row of half stitch. Simply make two half stitches with the workers and the edge pair before putting up the pin. A double half stitch is exactly the same as a cloth stitch and twist if you prefer to think of it in that way.

Fan. A triangular area with a curved side making an attractive headside for torchon edgings.

Footside. The usually straight edge on the right (in the UK) of an edging.

Gimp. A thick thread outlining part of a pattern.

Half Stitch. Number the positions of the bobbins from the left as usual. Lift 2 over 3, then 4 and 2 over 3 and 1 in the normal way.

Hanging on. There are two ways of hanging on two or more pairs around a pin to start a piece. To hang pairs on 'in order' push the first pair to the left and hang on the second pair to its right. The bobbins of each true pair will then lie next to each other. To hang pairs 'astride' or 'open' hang on the first pair with the bobbins close together, the next pair sits astride this pair with one bobbin outside each as shown below.

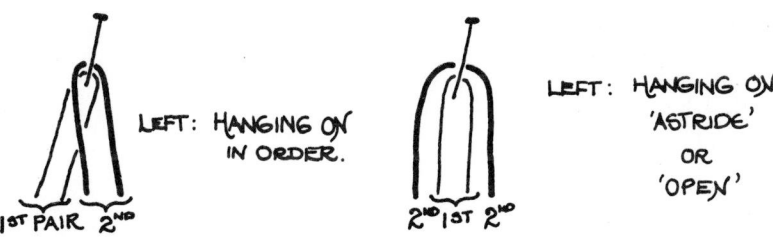

Headside. The curved or shaped edge on the left (in the UK) of an edging.

Interlinking. When starting a piece it is useful to interlink two pairs when they are hung from the same pin. This is done by hanging the first pair around the pin and pushing it to the left, the second pair is placed to its right and the two centre threads are twisted twice right over left as usual. This brings all the bobbins back to their true partner, but means that when the starting pin is removed the starting loops of each pair will be interlinked which will give a much neater effect.

Joining. At the end of a piece of work use a crochet hook or lazy susan to bring one thread of the finishing pair through the corresponding starting loop, remove the bobbin so that the thread can be pulled all the way through, replace the pin & tie off with a reef knot.

Passives. The pairs which go more or less straight down through the work at right angles to the workers.

Putting up a Pin. Pins should be pushed far enough into the pillow to prevent them wobbling when the threads around them are tensioned. Pins in the centre of the work should be upright or lean slightly backwards, they should NEVER slope forwards. The pins at the edges of a piece should lean slightly outwards. Pins can be pushed right down into the pillow to prevent them getting in the way at a later stage.

Reef Knots. Make an ordinary reef knot by passing the threads left over right and under and then right over left and under. This can be tied without removing the bobbins, in which case always hold the bobbins so that they can be passed spangle first through the loop. It is sometimes difficult to prevent the first half of the knot slackening whilst the second is made, to ensure that you do not lose the tension of the first part of the knot put an extra twist on the first half ie. left over right and under, over right and under again before pulling it tight.

A REEF KNOT

A REEF KNOT WITH AN EXTRA TWIST ON THE FIRST HALF

Sewing. 'Making a sewing' is a technique used to link two adjacent areas of work, usually two trails. The first trail is worked in the usual way, the second trail will share pinholes with the first so bring the worker pair to the shared pinhole and remove the pin. With a crochet hook or lazy susan bring ONE of the worker threads up through the loop formed by the workers at the edge of the first trail, pass the OTHER worker thread through the loop formed by its partner and replace the pin without splitting any of the threads. Tension the workers carefully before continuing.

Spider. A small cloth stitch oval with twisted pairs radiating out from it.

Tensioning. It is vital to tension your work at the end of each row before proceeding with the next row. To do this pull the worker tight and then tension each passive bobbin in turn so that all the threads lie smoothly and are evenly spread. Poor tensioning will spoil the appearance of your lace so its importance cannot be over-stressed.

Torchon Ground. There are several different combinations of stitches and twists which can be used to make up the more open net-like appearance of the background sections of the torchon pieces. I usually choose half stitch, pin, half stitch and twist, but you can easily substitute your favourite version if you prefer.

Trail. A narrow band or tape usually of cloth stitch.

Twist. Always lift the righthand bobbin over the left to twist a pair. The worker pair is usually twisted two or three times at the end of every row.

Weavers Knot. If you break a thread and need to use a knot to rejoin it this knot will enable you to trim the ends off very closely so that the knot is barely visible. Make a loop with the bobbin thread as shown, and pull a second loop through it, pass the broken end through that second loop and hold the two ends level. Now pull on the bobbin so that the bobbin thread tightens and forms the knot. Leave the ends as they are for as long as you can, trimming them short just before the knot goes into the work. Alternatively, having rejoined the broken thread, hang on a new bobbin and work it with the broken thread for 1/2" or so then throw out the knotted thread so that the knot does not actually go into the lace.

Winding Bobbins. Where I have given specific lengths of thread to use for projects it is obviously vital to wind half of each length onto each bobbin. To do this fold the length in half and trap the thread at the midpoint between the pillow and the pin by leaning the pin backwards at a very acute angle. Wind the thread by holding the bobbin in your left hand and winding AWAY from yourself. To make a hitch on the top of a bobbin wind the thread in the same direction twice around your left thumb. Place the tip of that thumb on the top of the bobbin and slip the loops down onto the head. Do not move your thumb until you have tightened the thread to hold it securely around the head of the bobbin. When you are using a very short length of thread you can attach it to the bobbin by making a simple slip knot and passing the head of the bobbin through the loop before pulling the thread tight. When you wish to remove the thread simply pull on the short end and the loop will grow large enough to allow you to slip the bobbin out.

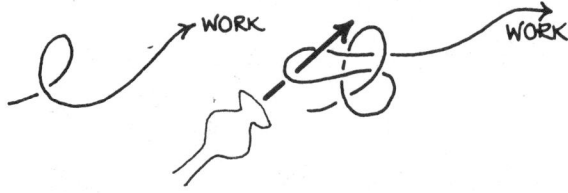

USING A SLIP KNOT TO ATTACH A SHORT LENGTH OF THREAD TO A BOBBIN.

Workers or Weavers. The pair which zig-zags from side to side of a cloth stitch or half stitch area.

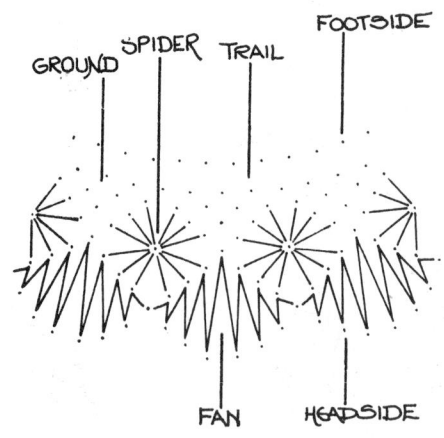

A PIECE OF LACE & THE PRICKING REQUIRED TO MAKE IT SHOWING THE BASIC FEATURES OF TORCHON LACE.

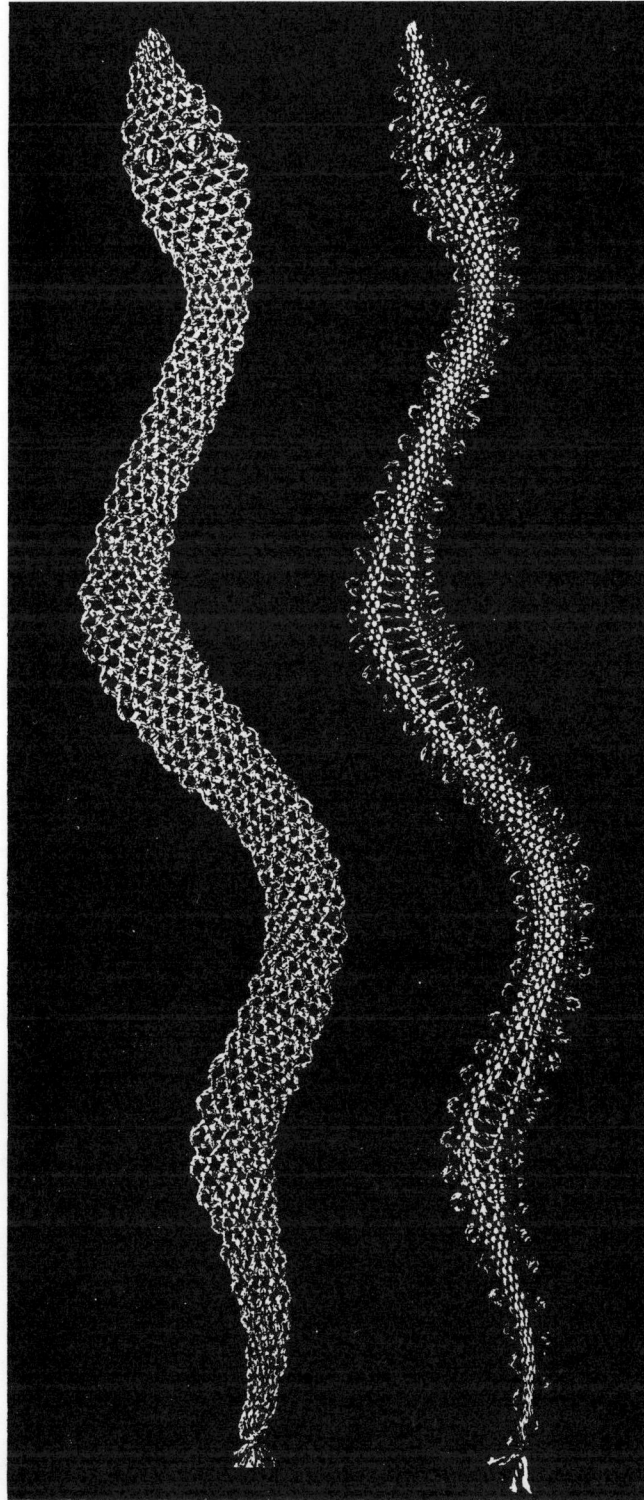

SNAKE BOOKMARK.

6 pairs of DMC Coton Perlé No 8 as passives. Cut 6 50" (125cm) lengths.
1 pair of Twilley's Gold Dust as workers. Cut 1 130" (325cm) length.
You will also need 2 3mm silver or gold metal beads.

This is a good beginner's project as it is a very colourful and glittery piece which makes it most attractive to children. Cloth stitch is used throughout and progress is generally quite rapid!

WORKING INSTRUCTIONS.

I use six different colours for the passive threads and usually try to arrange for the darker colours to come at the edges. We have seen some attractive snakes with silver or gold workers, but a green glittery thread definitely seems to be the most popular and effective. As usual it is important to divide each thread into two and wind half onto each bobbin of the pair. Try to avoid putting a pin through the mid-point of the thread, instead trap the thread between the pillow and a pin which has been placed in the pillow at a very acute angle. This prevents the thread from becoming split and worn. Winding such a long length of thick, glittery thread onto the worker bobbins is a tricky task. Choose a pair of bobbins with the longest possible neck to give the greatest thread capacity and wind on the thread evenly and tightly. This thread does tend to make the hitch jump off the head of the bobbin, therefore it is often better to make just a single hitch which is positioned on top of the thread, rather than in the higher indentation on the head of the bobbin.

Hang the worker pair on the 'nose-pin' of the snake and push the bobbins to the left. Hang on the passives one pair at a time pushing each pair to the left before adding the next. Cloth stitch the workers through all the passives and twist them twice at the end of this and every row. Put up the pin between the workers and the passives and tension each pair carefully. Continue in cloth stitch doing your best to keep the outside passive pair as close to the edge pins as possible, tension them by pulling them well out to the side rather than pulling them straight down the pillow which will give you a very 'thin' head.

Leave your workers at the beginning of the row on which the eyes are marked and put on the beads using the second and fifth pairs of passives. I use a fine piece of wire which has been folded in half and pinched tightly together (alternatively you can use a lazy susan or a crochet hook if the hole in the bead is large enough). Pass one end of the wire underneath one of the passive threads and push the thread down into the bend in the wire. Put the ends of wire together and thread on the bead. Pull the wire through the bead easing the doubled passive through behind it. Hold the loop of thread which has been pulled through the bead carefully and disengage the wire, now pass the other bobbin of that pair through the loop. Gently, pulling evenly on both threads swing the bobbins wide apart and the bead will slide up the threads and position itself close against the work. Do exactly the same for the other eye. Now continue with the cloth stitch.

As the body of the snake begins to widen, introduce a twist on the workers between the third and fourth pairs of passives. At first this is only one twist, but it gradually increases to three and then slowly decreases again back to solid cloth stitch with twists only at the ends of each row. It is important to make sure that the centre twists are always made in the correct direction (ie. right worker bobbin over left worker bobbin). The twists are increased again as the body widens lower down.

Watch out for accidental twists on the passives. These are usually immediately obvious if the colour order of the passives is upset, but if two threads of the same colour are twisted it is harder to spot, however even if uncorrected it is unlikely to spoil the overall effect.

Good tensioning is essential throughout as unless the passives are well-straightened at the end of every row they will tend to turn your smooth-skinned snake into a lumpy, bumpy caterpillar. The Perlé thread is strong and usually survives quite well, more care is required with the glittery workers which will snap under too much pressure.

At the end of the tail don't twist the workers before putting up the final pin, now take the lower worker thread back through the passives undoing that part of the row. Once it has reached the other edge, take a glitter thread in each hand and tie a collecting knot to bring all the threads tightly together. Trim the threads quite close to the knot if you intend to put the snake in a plastic sleeve, and use some of the leftover pieces of thread to make a tassel to put through a hole which you punch in the end of the sleeve. If it is not to go into a plastic sleeve you might like to leave a longer tassel of thread below the collecting knot.

If you like you can use exactly the same pattern and work it in half stitch.

6 pairs of Twilley's Gold Dust, either in a single colour or a variety. Cut 6 60" (150cm) lengths.

Wind the bobbins as before and hang all the pairs from the tip of the snake's nose. The entire snake is worked in half stitch, with two extra twists being added at the end of every row to ensure the worker thread changes each time. The eyes are added in just the same way, but obviously no extra twists are added as the body widens, the half stitch pattern of threads will shape itself to accommodate the extra width in a very attractive way.

The finished snake can be wriggled into a plastic sleeve where it makes a handsome bookmark for a young reader, or a welcome gift for an older bookworm!

SIMPLE TORCHON CANDLE.

6 pairs of Twilley's Gold Dust in gold. Cut 6 42" (110cm) lengths.
2 pairs of Twilley's Gold Dust in red. Cut 2 48" (125cm) lengths.
2 pairs of Twilley's Gold Dust in green. Cut 2 36" (90cm) lengths.

There are two versions of this pattern, in one the candle consists entirely of torchon ground stitches, in the other there are three spiders, which is obviously a little more difficult. Both have half stitch flames, so this project gives an excellent opportunity to practise torchon ground and half stitch. It should be easy for the child to spot any mistakes in the main part of the candle as the coloured threads will move diagonally through the torchon ground only changing direction when they reach the outside edge or become part of the spider.

**Opposite: Left: Candle made entirely in torchon ground.
Right: Candle with three spiders & torchon ground.**

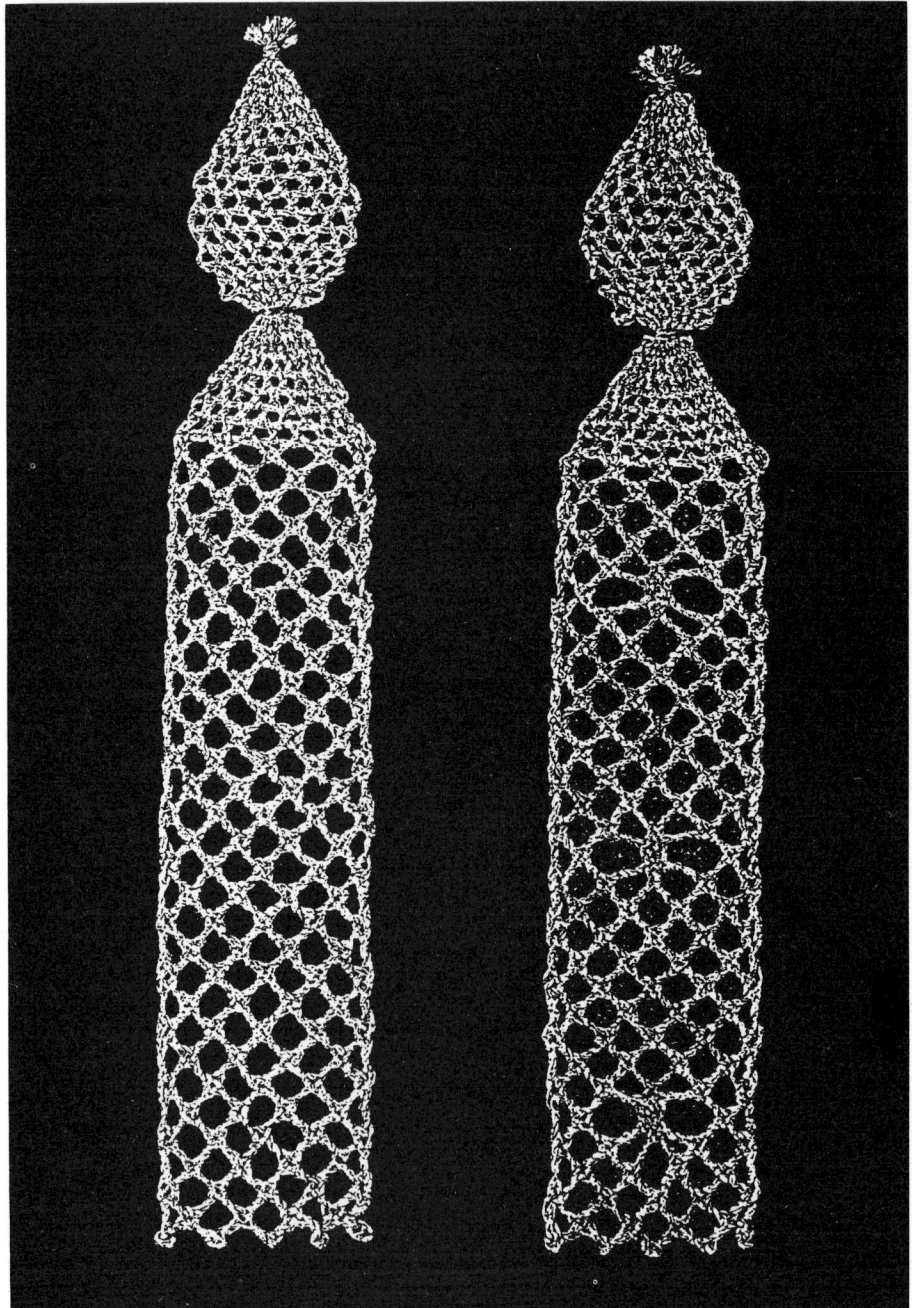

WORKING INSTRUCTIONS.

Divide each length of thread in half and wind on the bobbins. The pricking is pinned to the pillow with the flame of the candle nearest to you. Put a pin into each of the top row of pinholes — five in all. Starting at the lefthand end of that row of five pins hang two pairs of bobbins on every pin. On pin 1 hang 1 gold and then 1 green, on pin 2 hang 2 gold, on pin 3 hang 2 red, on pin 4 hang 2 gold, on pin 5 hang 1 green and then one gold. Now interlink each pair by twisting the middle two threads (of the 4 hanging from each pin) twice (twist them right over left as usual). Now twist every pair twice.

Take the green pair from pin 1 and the lefthand gold pair from pin 2 and make a torchon ground stitch (half stitch, pin, half stitch and twist both pairs once) putting up pin 6. Pin 7 at the edge will be worked with two gold pairs in exactly the same way. Now go back up to pin 8 which is worked with the gold pair from pin 2 and the lefthand red pair from pin 3. Continue working down the diagonal line until you reach pin 11, the red pair will have worked down through the whole line. Return to pin 4 to start the next diagonal row (pins 12-17). The green pair from pin 5 will work pin 18 with the gold pair from pin 4 at the start of the next diagonal row. If you are not intending to include the three spiders in your piece you will continue to work towards the lefthand edge pin 25, before going back to the righthand edge to start the next diagonal row. Working entire rows in this way should ensure that your coloured threads follow the correct pathways. With very inexperienced children it may be worth actually drawing coloured lines onto the card pricking to indicate where the red and green threads should go.

If you are going to work the three spiders then you will work as far as pin 20, leave the two pairs hanging from this pin and return to the two righthand-most pairs to work pins 21, 22, & 23. Again return to the righthand edge and work pins 24 & 25, then edge pin 26. Now you can work your spider. Firstly make a cloth stitch with the two pairs of green

Working diagrams for Simple Torchon Candles:-
Left: Candle with torchon ground   Right: Candle with spiders

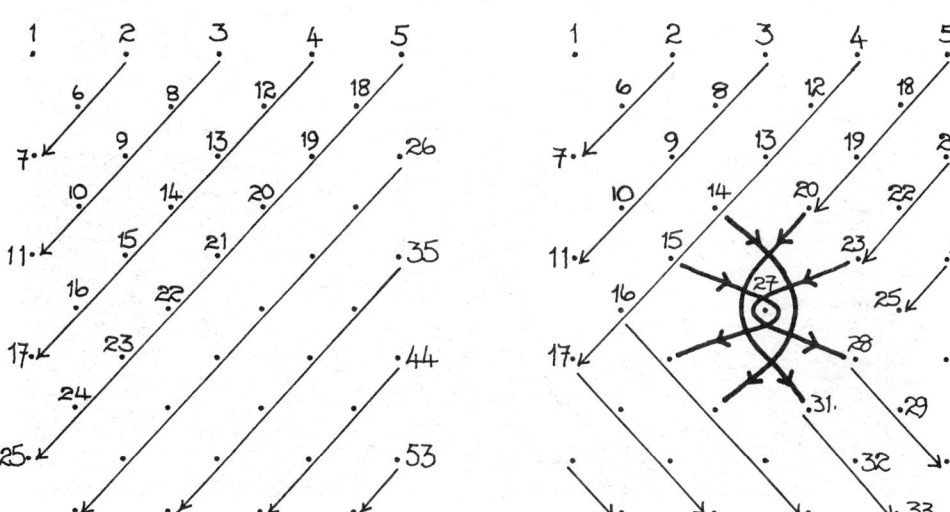

threads in the centre, now work a cloth stitch with the righthand green pair and the gold pair to its right. Work a similar cloth stitch with the lefthand green pair and the gold pair to its left. Finally work a cloth stitch with the two gold pairs which are now in the centre. Put up pin 27 in the centre of the spider's body and tension all the threads. Now repeat the previous four cloth stitches, but in reverse order — ie. A cloth stitch with the two gold pairs, two cloth stitches with one gold and one green pair and finally a cloth stitch with the two green pairs. This completes the body of the spider, but you now need to add two twists to each of the four pairs coming out of its body to make its legs. (There was no need to add extra twists to the pairs forming the top four spider legs as each pair was already twisted twice from the half stitch and twist of the torchon ground).

Return to making diagonal rows of torchon ground starting with pins 28, 29 & 30, followed by 31-34. Restart the next row from pin 16 and work it all the way down to the righthand edge. The next row starts from pin 17. Continue your work until you reach the final horizontal row of pins which should be worked with a cloth stitch above each pin (do not cover the pin). Twist the gold pair on the left of the work once and half stitch it across the row. At the end of the row twist the 'workers' once if the last thread you worked through was red or green, and twice if it was gold. This will ensure that it is always a gold thread which works from one side of the row to the other.

When you reach the narrowest point (the top of the candle and the base of the flame) take the two outside threads (both red if you have done your half stitch correctly) and make a collecting knot. This is done by tying the first half of a reef knot with an extra twist on top of the threads (the extra twist prevents the knotting threads slipping loose before you can tie the rest of the knot). Pass the righthand knotting thread under all the passives to its left by lifting each bobbin in turn to keep them in the same order. Do exactly the same with the lefthand knotting thread, now tie another reef knot on top of the work pulling the knot as tight as possible. Throw back the four green threads as they will not be used in the flame.

Start the half stitch flame by twisting the two lefthand threads once (one red and one gold thread) so that the red thread lies inside the gold and half stitch across. In order to make a nice red flame keep a red thread as your weaver by twisting once at the end of a row if you wish to keep the same worker, and twice if you wish to change it. If you twist twice then the last thread you worked through will become your new worker. You will finish your flame with the worker on the right. Take the two outside threads and tie a collecting knot in the same way as you did at the base of the flame. This time there is no need to keep all the passives in order, so you simply pick up all the bobbins in a bunch in order to pass the two knotting threads underneath them. Trim the passives about ¼" (6mm) away from the knot, and the knotting threads a little closer. Trim the green threads off close to the reef knot at the base of the flame.

It is advisable to leave your finished candle pinned to the pillow for twenty four hours before removing the pins. Then it can be slipped inside a plastic sleeve as a bookmark, or if you prefer it can be glued to the front of a Christmas card. If you are making it into a bookmark then trim the plastic sleeve to give a clear ¾"-1" (2.25cm) below the lace. Use a leather or hole punch to make a hole in the centre of the sleeve about ¼" (6mm) in from the lower edge. Select six or so left-over pieces of thread at least 8" (20cm) long and fold them in half. Pull the folded loop through the hole in the cover and open the loop so that the ends can be pushed through and pulled tight to form a tassel. Trim the ends level about 1½" (3.5cm) away from the knot.

TORCHON CANDLE.

This is quite a challenging piece for a child including spiders, ground and cloth stitch diamonds. The top section of the candle is worked in half stitch, the flame is also worked in half stitch with a double half stitch at the edge to outline the flame.

12 pairs of DMC Coton Perlé No 8. Cut 12 108" (300cm) lengths.
 2 pairs of Twilley's Gold Dust. Cut 2 108" (300cm) lengths.

Take one pair of Perlé bobbins and hang them from T1, take a second pair and hang it from the same pin putting it down to the right of the previous pair. Twist the centre two bobbins twice (right over left as usual). The bobbins have returned to their original positions, but the threads are now interlinked. Twist the righthand pair twice and then the lefthand pair twice. Hang two Perlé pairs from each of pins T2, 3, 5, 6 & 7, and the two glittery pairs from T4. Interlink and twist each pair twice in exactly the same way as at T1.

Work torchon ground (half stitch, pin, half stitch and twist both pairs once) for the triangular areas on each side of the diamond (pins 8-19 & 20-31). You will find that the glittery pairs go straight along the diagonals from their starting point in the centre to the edges of the lace.

Work the cloth stitch diamond next taking great care to tension the threads really well at the end of every row. You must also remember to include a new pair at the end of every row as the diamond gets wider (pins 32-42) and to leave out a pair from each of pins 41-50 as the diamond gets narrower. One pair will come into the diamond above and leave the diamond immediately below pins 41 & 42. At every other pinhole on the edge of the diamond you will EITHER have one pair coming in OR one pair going out.

Work the triangles of torchon ground below the diamond (pins 52-69 & 70-87). Now work the spider which has two twists on every leg. If you have worked everything correctly you will find that the glittery pair will run round the edge of the spider's body. Don't forget to put 2 twists on each leg before continuing with the ground (pins 89-106 & 107-124). Repeat from the start of the cloth stitch diamond (pin 32).

Complete the final row of torchon ground making one slightly different stitch at pin A — instead of doing half stitches here do a cloth stitch, pin, cloth stitch. Take the righthand pair from pin A as your workers and half stitch across to pin B, add 2 extra twists and continue in half stitch until you have reached pin K1. You will find that the one thread which goes all the way across from one side to the other of each row will change each time. This should ensure that your threads are used more or less evenly, but should a thread run short then you can vary the number of twists on the worker pair in order to control which thread works the full width of the row. To do this make sure that the bobbin (of the two workers) with more thread is the one left nearest the pin once all the twists are in place, if it is not then remove one twist.

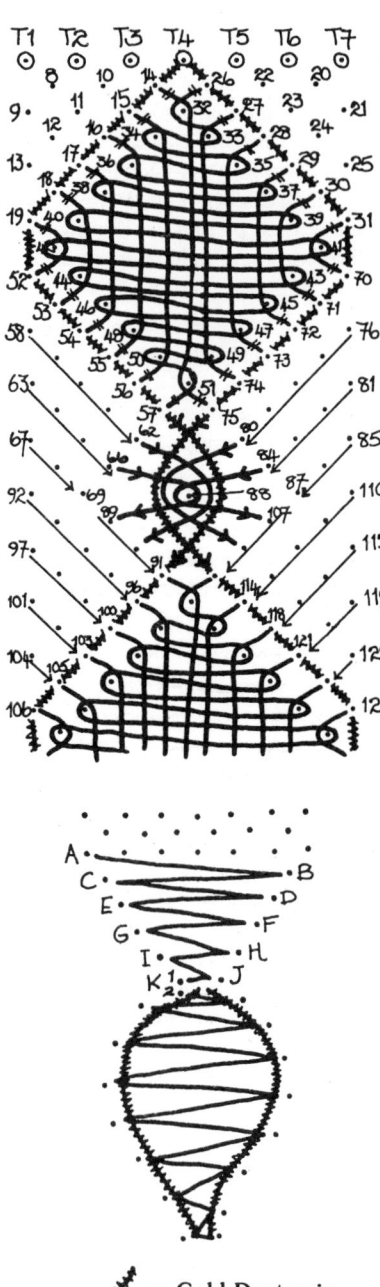

Prickings for Simple Torchon Candles

Working Diagrams for Torchon Candle

Take the lefthand bobbin of the worker pair which is outside pin K1, and take the righthand bobbin from the opposite side of the work to tie a collecting knot. (Tie the first half of a reef knot with these two threads, but put an extra twist on the first half of the knot. Pull it tight, then lift the bobbins in turn keeping the passive threads strictly in order whilst you pass the right hand knot bobbin under all the passives until it lies on the left, and then the lefthand knot thread so that it lies on the right. Now tie an ordinary reef knot on top of the work using the same two threads and pulling the knot as tight as possible.) When tying these knots always pick up the bobbins in such a way that they can be passed spangle first through the thread loops, you'll find that the beads are much less of a problem in this way!

Put up pin K2 between the two lefthand bobbins and the rest of the passives. Move the glittery pairs, which should have made a neat oval shape through the centre of the half stitch section, from their positions in the centre of the work to lie just to the right of pin K2 and on the right of all the passives at the opposite edge. Tension all the pairs really well before continuing. Work the flame in half stitch, but put on an extra half stitch every time you come to a glittery pair. This can be called a double half stitch or you can think of it as a cloth stitch and twist which is exactly the same thing. Add two extra twists to the workers at the end of every row making a total of three twists on those threads before putting up the pin.

At the tip of the flame put up the last pin and make a collecting knot with the glittery threads (this time there is no need to keep the passives in order, so you can simply bunch them together when you lift them to pass the knotting threads underneath). Take care when tying this knot with the glitter threads as they are not as strong as the Perlé ones. Tension all the threads for the last time then trim all the ends about ¼" (6mm) away from the knot and remove the pins.

This piece can be slipped into a plastic sleeve to make a bookmark. Once the lace is inside trim the sleeve if necessary and punch a hole in the centre about ¼" (6mm) in from the lower edge. Take some of the leftover thread from the candle and sort out those pieces which are at least 6" (15cm) long, and arrange them so that one end of all the threads is level. Place another piece of Perlé thread across those threads about 3" (7.5cm) away from the level ends, fold the threads back on themselves to lie on top of this piece. Thread the ends of the single piece of Perlé through the hole in the sleeve and pull until the folded loop of the bunch of threads follows. Continue pulling until the loop is big enough to enable you to open it wide and push all the ends through. Pull your tassel tight and trim off all the ends to an even length about 1½-2" (4-5cm) away from the bottom edge of the sleeve.

If you prefer, your candle can be mounted as a Christmas card using a piece of card 8" x 8¼" (20cm x 20.5cm) which is folded in half to give a finished size of 4" x 8¼" (10cm x 20.5cm). You can use commercial gold or silver holly leaves to match the glittery pair in the lace, or you can cut out felt holly leaves and berries. Red 8mm 'cup' sequins make excellent berries.

Far Right: Finished Torchon Candle
Right: Pricking for Torchon Candle
Below: Finished card showing Torchon Candle with holly leaves and six 8mm 'cup' sequins as berries.

A CRINOLINE LADY.

6 pairs of DMC 80 Cordonnet Special. Cut 6 4 yard (4m) lengths.
1 pair of DMC Fil a Dentelle in a contrasting colour. Cut 1 18" (45cm) length.

A useful piece to test or revise the mastery of a wide variety of techniques. With care it could be used as a beginner's piece for an adult or teenager.

WORKING INSTRUCTIONS.

Start at the neck edge of the centre front strip and hang two pairs of passives 'in order' on each of pins T1 and T2, the workers should be hung on pin T3. Cloth stitch across and twist the workers twice at the end of the row before putting up the pin. Remove pins T1 and T2 and tension all the pairs carefully. Continue in cloth stitch twisting twice at the end of every row until you reach pin A.

At pin A the passives will be divided into two groups with two pairs in each. Cloth stitch through the first two pairs of passives, twist the workers twice and put up pin B, cloth stitch back to pin C twisting the workers twice as usual. Work back through the same two pairs of passives and put up pin D, then back to pin E in the same way. After putting up pin E cloth stitch through the first two pairs of passives, twist the workers once and complete the row by cloth stitching through the remaining two pairs of passives and putting up pin F. Continue in cloth stitch with one twist in the centre of the row until you reach pin G.

After pin G cloth stitch through the first two pairs of passives, twist the workers twice and put up pin H, work back to pin I, then to pin J and back to pin K using cloth stitch all the time and remembering to twist twice at the end of every row. At this point you will change to half stitch, so put one twist on each of the four passives and continue in half stitch with two additional twists at the end of every row until you reach pin T3 which was the starting pin for your original workers at the neckline. Make a sewing into the loop of thread at T3 using your current workers, replace the pin and tension the threads carefully. Hang the coloured thread from pin M and return to your workers. Half stitch the workers across to pin M making a double half stitch (or a cloth stitch and twist) with the contrasting coloured pair at the outer edge of the bonnet. Add two more twists to the white workers (making a total of three altogether) and remove pin M to put it up again in the usual way (between the workers and all the rest of the passives). Continue in half stitch with the double stitch at the outside edge only until you reach pin 4.

Make a sewing with your workers into pin 4 and tie off the coloured threads with a reef knot throwing the bobbins back out of the way. Continue in cloth stitch. At pin N add a twist to the workers between the outside passives and the other three pairs. At pin O maintaining the twist between the first two pairs introduce a twist between the second and third pairs. At P also twist the workers between the third and fourth pairs of passives. Continue twisting the workers in this way until you reach pin Q.

Working through only the outer edge two pairs of passives (and maintaining the twist between them) work pins R1, S, R2 and T. Work across all four pairs of passives to put up pins U, V & W, twisting the workers once between every pair of passives. Now work only through the inner two pairs of passives for pins X1, A, X2 & C, making sewings with your workers into pins A & C. Work back through the first three pairs of passives towards pin

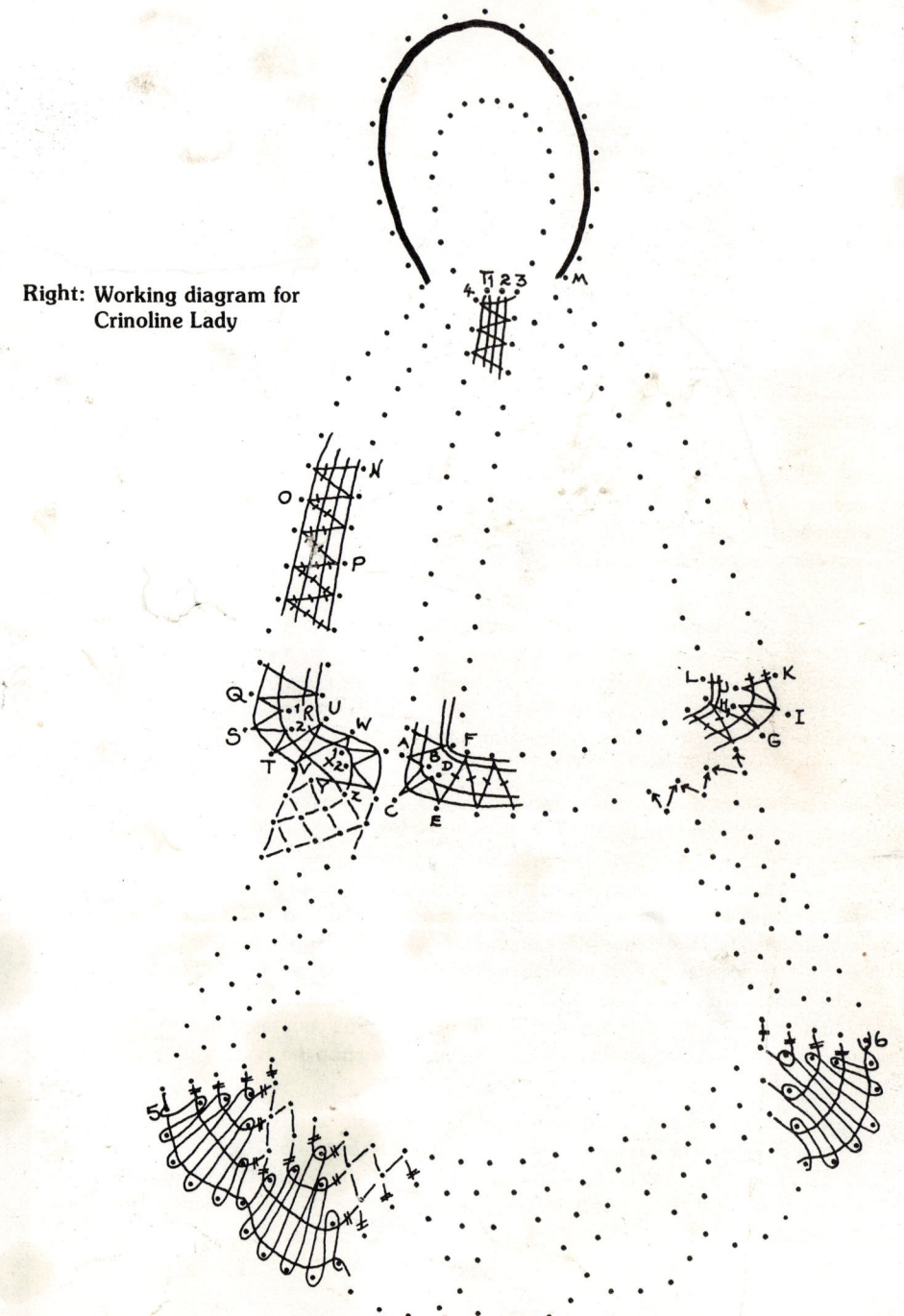

Right: Working diagram for Crinoline Lady

Y. Hang a new pair of bobbins onto pin Y and make a torchon ground stitch (half stitch, pin, half stitch and twist) with the new pair and the old workers. (You will need to take out pin Y and reposition it after completing the first half stitch part of that torchon ground stitch.) Twist the outside passive hanging from pin V once and make a ground stitch at the edge pin. Take the passive pair from X2 and the pair to its left and make a ground stitch at Z. With the lefthand pair from Z complete the diagonal row of ground towards your left until it reaches the edge. Now go back to the innermost edge and take the passive pair hanging inside pin C and the righthand pair from pin Z and make a ground stitch at the innermost edge pin. Continue in diagonal rows of ground until you reach the corner of the skirt.

Put up pin 5 between the outermost two pairs of passives, twist the lefthand pair once more and it now becomes your workers for the fan. Work the fan in cloth stitch twisting the workers twice at the end of every row, taking in a new pair from the ground as the fan gets wider and leaving a pair out as it gets narrower. Put two twists on each of the three pairs dropping out of the fan, now complete the triangular area of torchon ground before starting the next fan. Continue along the hem of the skirt, you can if you wish introduce more variety of stitches into the treatment of the fans. Put up the pin at the end of the last fan and make a half stitch beneath it before putting up pin 6. Complete the ground stitch at pin 6 with another half stitch and twist. Make sure that all the pairs coming out of the fan are twisted twice then complete the first diagonal row in torchon ground stitch. If you would like to use a slightly different ground stitch for the second side of the skirt, try cloth stitch, pin, cloth stitch and twist for a change.

Continue until the skirt meets the edge of the cloak. Complete the last row of pinholes and then sew the pairs into the corresponding pinholes of the cloak. Tie the ends with a reef knot and trim them off close to the knots, also trim off the coloured thread at the side of the bonnet. Remove all the pins and turn your lady over so that the right side is uppermost. Complete her bonnet by adding a small bow tied in DMC Coton Perlé No 8 in a colour to match that edging her bonnet.

Use your crinoline lady to decorate a card or notelet, or frame her for all to admire! I used a 7" x 5" (18cm x 13cm) photo frame with a 5" x 3½" (12.5cm x 9cm) oval mount. (In fact I used the paper mount supplied in the frame cutting along the inside edge of the oval marking to remove the centre section on which were printed all the size details, to make a most attractive setting for the lady.)

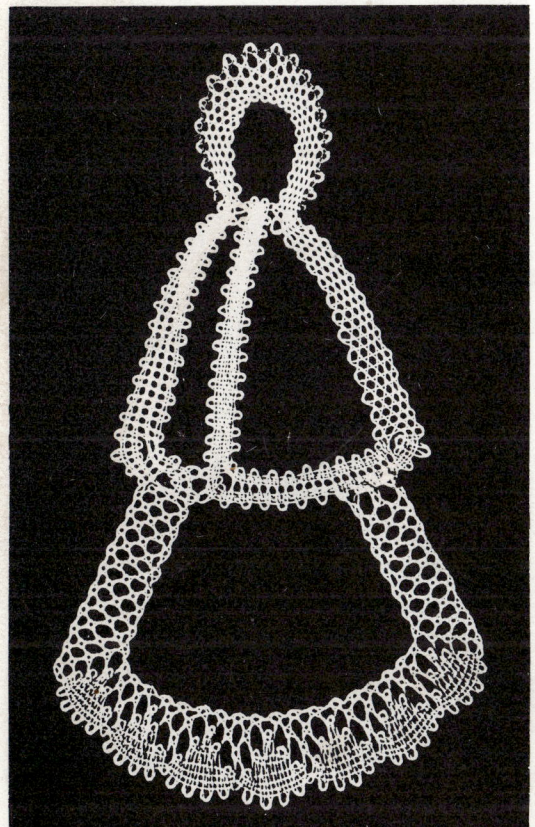
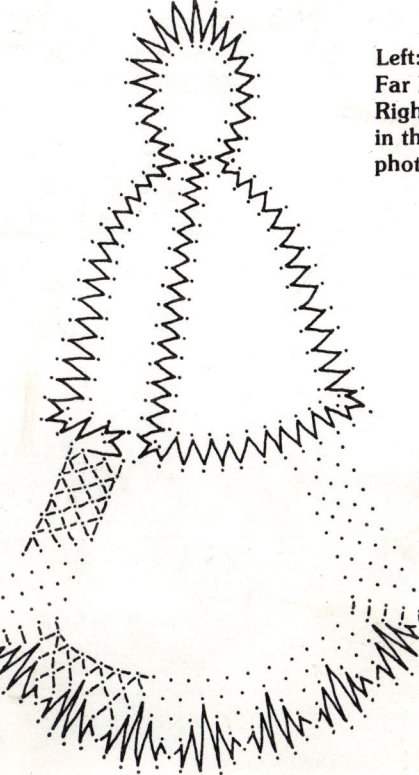

Left: Pricking for Crinoline Lady
Far Left: Finished Lace
Right: Crinoline Lady mounted in the oval cut-out of a photograph frame.

SIMPLE FLOWERS.

These can be made in three sizes using DMC Coton Perlé No 8, Twilley's Gold Dust or a combination of both.

Small — Cloth stitch - 4 pairs of passives. Cut 4 14" (35cm) lengths.
                       1 pair of workers. Cut 1 50" (125cm) length.
        Half stitch - 4 pairs. Cut 4 20" (50cm) lengths.

Medium — Cloth stitch - 6 pairs of passives. Cut 6 18" (45cm) lengths.
                        1 pair of workers. Cut 1 80" (200cm) length.
         Half stitch - 6 pairs. Cut 6 24" (60cm) lengths.
                        1 pair as an additional outside passive if required.

Large — Cloth stitch - 7 pairs of passives. Cut 7 20" (50cm) lengths.
                       1 pair of workers. Cut 1 90" (225cm) length.
        Half stitch - 7 pairs. Cut 7 26" (65cm) lengths.
                       1 pair as an additional outside passive if required.

The lengths of thread required for the passives of all the flowers are quite short to avoid wasting a lot of thread, so it is essential to tie them onto the bobbin before you start winding them or they will soon be slipping to the floor as there is insufficient thread to wind on top of the end to keep it in place in the usual way. Either use two or three half hitches around the neck of the bobbin, or making a loop use the bobbin like a crochet hook to go down through the loop and bring up a second loop of thread around its neck, as if you were starting to crochet a chain. Pull the thread tight around the bobbin and wind on the thread as usual. When you wish to remove the thread simply pull on the very end of it and the loop around the bobbin's neck will magically grow larger and allow you to slip the bobbin out quite easily.

WORKING INSTRUCTIONS FOR THE SMALL FLOWER.

Hang two pairs of passives on each of pins T1 and T2. Hang the worker on pin 3. Cloth stitch across through three pairs of passives, twisting the workers once before cloth stitching through the outermost passive. Twist the workers twice at the end of every row and put up the pin. After two rows remove pins T1 and T2 and tension the passives carefully.

Because younger children may find it difficult to remember to twist the workers inside the outer passive pair it does help if that edge pair is a different colour from the other three passives, there is then a clear division between the two groups of passives.

Check that the twists are done in the correct way — right over left, and that there are no accidental twists on the passives. To help avoid this you can set up the passives in pairs of alternate coloured bobbins. It is important to tension well at the end of every row to give your flower a nice smooth surface.

At the end bring the workers to the inside edge but don't twist them. Put up the final pin and slip the lefthand worker underneath the pin instead of above it. With one worker thread above the pin and one below it tie a reef knot with an extra twist on the first half around the final pin. Do not trim either of these ends as they will be needed to gather up your flower and stitch it together.

If the outer passive is a different colour then it helps to bring those two bobbins to the centre of the passives before knotting them and trimming them off. To do this put the two contrasting coloured threads together and pass them under and over each of the four passive threads to their right. Tie each passive pair in a reef knot leaving the contrasting coloured pair until last. Trim the passives close to the knots.

Remove the worker bobbins and take out all the pins. Now thread a needle with the longer of the two worker threads and stab stitch this up and down through the loops along the straight edge. Pull this gathering thread as tight as possible and secure it with a double backstitch. Lap the starting edge over the knots of the finishing edge and again stab stitch the neater end into place. Fasten off the sewing thread well and then trim off both of the two remaining threads. (Although you are only going to use one of the worker threads to do the gathering and to stitch the flower together, do not be tempted to trim off the shorter thread before you have completed the flower, as the strain of pulling the gathering thread tight could work the reef knot at the end of the lace undone and cause all sorts of problems!)

If you wish you can use exactly the same pattern and work it in half stitch, in which case hang one pair on T1, two on T2 and the fourth on pin 3, which will start off as the worker. Put two additional twists on the worker at the end of every row to ensure that it changes each time. Make up the flower in exactly the same way as described above.

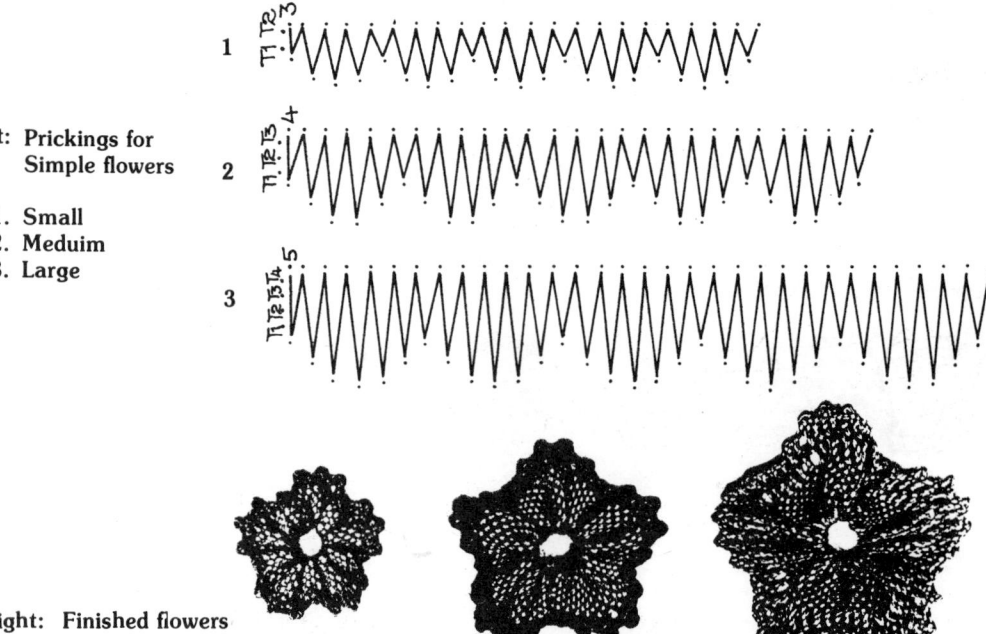

Right: Prickings for Simple flowers
1. Small
2. Meduim
3. Large

Right: Finished flowers

WORKING INSTRUCTIONS FOR THE MEDIUM FLOWER.

This is worked in a very similar way to the smaller flower. There will be three temporary pins along the top edge with two pairs on each pin. You will work through five pairs of passives before putting a twist on the workers and cloth stitching through the outer passive pair which may be of a contrasting colour. The flower is completed in exactly the same way as before.

In the half stitch version you must hang the passives across the top edge of the strip with one pair, which will start off as the worker, on the pin at the top of the straight edge and the outer passive, should you choose to have one, at the left of the temporary pins, closest to the scalloped edge. If you have included the extra passive pair in a contrasting colour you must remember to work a double half stitch (ie. two half stitches, or a cloth stitch and twist) every time you come to work through that pair so that it remains at the outer edge. At the other end of the row you will put two extra twists as usual onto the worker pair before putting up the pin.

WORKING INSTRUCTIONS FOR THE LARGE FLOWER.

Hang one pair of passives on T1, two pairs of passives on each of T2, T3 and T4, and the worker on pin 5. Cloth stitch across and put one twist on the workers between the fifth and sixth pair of passives and also the sixth and seventh pair on every row. There are two twists as usual on the worker at the end of each row.

This pattern can be worked in half stitch with or without a contrasting coloured edge pair. If it is included then you must remember to do a double half stitch every time you work it so that it stays at the outer edge. Add two twists to the worker at the end of every row as usual.

Both flowers are completed in exactly the same way as the smaller flowers.

SUGGESTED COLOUR COMBINATIONS.

Obviously there are many different colour possibilities, but one of the most successful is to choose a lighter group of passives for the inner, solid part of the flower and to have the outer passive and the worker a darker shade. Alternatively use all one colour with just the outer pair of passives in a stronger shade or a completely contrasting colour. Enjoy experimenting and making your own combinations.

Finished lace for all three sizes of flower

PROJECTS USING ONE SMALL FLOWER.

Glue one small flower into the corner of one side of a gift box, or take a piece of card 2" x 4" (5cm x 10cm), fold it in half to make a gift tag and stick one flower into the bottom righthand corner. Slip two small leaves under the edge of the petals and glue them into place. Use a metallic gold or silver felt pen to write your greeting onto the card or add a ready-made message such as "Best Wishes" for a really professional finish.

Gift tag using one small flower and two tiny leaves

Gift box decoration using one small flower and two leaves

PROJECTS USING TWO SMALL FLOWERS.

You can trim a pair of ear-rings by simply gluing the flowers in place, or you can make a small spray of flowers which can decorate the front of a Mother's Day or special birthday card, and then be removed to wear on the lapel of a jacket.

The spray consists of two small flowers made in cloth stitch and a ready-made leaf. I chose a five-sectioned leaf as you can see in the illustration. Take a piece of fine florist's wire (or brass spangling wire) and thread it through some of the gathers on the back of the flower, try to go through at least three folds in the gathers around the centre hole of the flower, bend the wire round and bring the ends together. Take just two pairs of stamens and position them carefully in the centre of the flower, now twist the ends of the wire and the stamens together. Trim off the ends about 2" (5cm) away from the flower. With florist's tape you can cover the twisted wire and stamens to form a nice green stem. Do the same for the second flower, but make a shorter stem — about 1¼" (3cm).

Position the two flowers on top of the leaf and wind a short length of florist's tape around the stems of both the leaf and the flowers to keep them in place. Now shape the leaf, curving the central wire to give it a more natural appearance and if necessary bend the stems of the flowers to achieve an attractive arrangement.

If you would like to mount this on a card, then those with a cut out shape in the centre look most effective. Choose a neutral coloured card in white, cream or beige, and taking a contrasting coloured piece of card which will go well with the colours you chose for the flowers, cut a piece small enough to slip behind and completely cover the cut out shape. Hold the spray diagonally in the centre of the cut out shape and make two small pencil spots one on each side of the stems, level with the lowest edge of the lower flower. Using a hole punch make two small holes in the coloured card at these points and thread a length of narrow ribbon down through the first hole and up through the second, to tie the spray in place with a bow. Trim the ribbon ends as necessary. Glue the coloured background card into place using a few spots of glue at the edge of the card. The ribbon can easily be untied and the spray removed for wear. Use a gold or silver pen to write your message or greeting.

Even the youngest lacemaker can make a reasonable job of the little flowers, the gathering will hide any small mistakes, but obviously the younger child will need an adult's help, or that of an older child, to assemble the spray and mount it onto the card.

A spray of two small flowers which can be used to decorate a card (right)

PROJECTS USING A VARIETY OF FLOWERS.

It is possible to make a number of flowers of different sizes and use them in a wide variety of projects.

AN ALICE BAND.

Make one large, one medium and one small flower. I used a combination of two shades of pink DMC Perlé and pink Twilley's Gold Dust. The smallest flower has 3 dark pink passives, a pale pink worker and a glittery pink outer passive. The medium flower has a dark pink outside passive and worker with five pairs of glittery inner passives. The largest flower has a pale pink worker, five pairs of dark pink passives and two outer passives of pink Gold Dust.

The flowers are glued onto a wide Alice band with four small green 'rose' leaves. Obviously the number of flowers and the arrangement can be varied considerably, and if you prefer they can be glued onto a hair comb or stitched onto corded ribbon as a hairband rather than onto a rigid plastic Alice band.

Three sets of earrings showing how the smallest flowers can be used to decorate a variety of inexpensive earrings

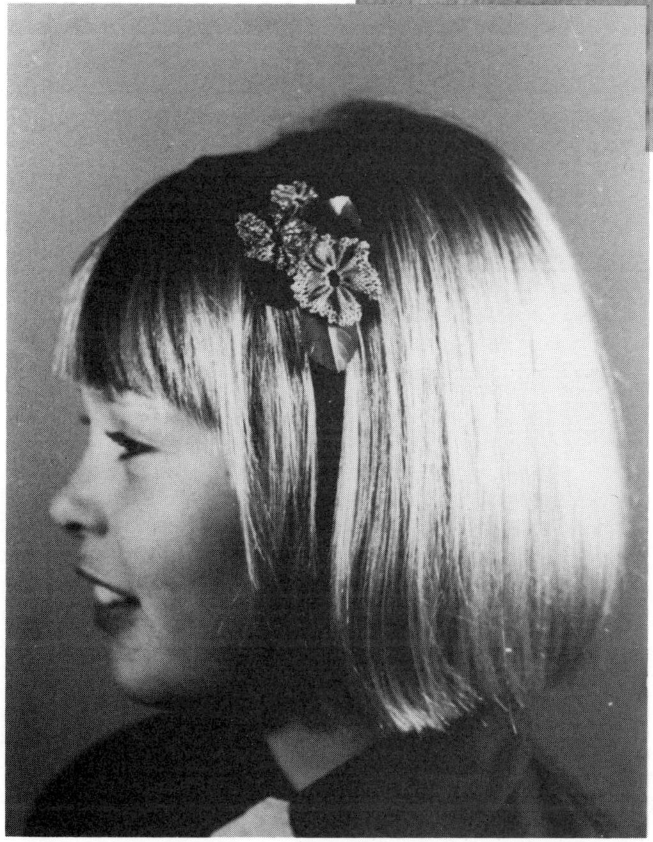

Left & above: A group of three flowers & leaves decorating an Alice Band

Above: 4 small & 1 large flower together with three leaves make up an attractive corsage.

A CORSAGE.

I used three of the smallest flowers made in various shades of purples, mauves and pinks. The larger flower is made up of one small flower stitched or glued onto the top of a larger one which can be made in either half stitch or cloth stitch. If you choose to work it in half stitch use a contrasting coloured edge passive which is worked with a double half stitch (cloth stitch and twist) so that it always stays at the curved edge of the petals.

Each flower is completed and assembled in the usual way, wired with fine florist's wire and covered with green florist's tape to make the stem. You can add stamens to each flower if you like. I used three large 'rose' leaves with a silky green fabric type finish as a background for my spray. When you have arranged the leaves and flowers to your satisfaction wind more green tape around the stems to keep them firmly in place. You can now make minor adjustments by bending the flower stems and curving the leaves to give a more natural appearance.

CARDS FOR ALL OCCASIONS.

These very simple flowers can be used in a wide variety of ways to decorate greeting cards. I hope that the following suggestions will give you some ideas on which to base your own designs.

WEDDING AND ANNIVERSARY CARDS.

The simplest card uses one medium and one small flower which are worked entirely in silver Twilley's Gold Dust, some small silver leaves, two silver flower-shaped sequins and a commercial heart motif and 'Congratulations'. This can be mounted on a background card of any appropriate colour, but looks particularly effective on red to make a lovely Ruby Wedding Card.

For a Silver Wedding card use four small flowers, one medium and one large flower. All are made in white DMC Perlé with a pair of silver Gold Dust outer passives. Blue card fills the oval cut out providing a good background for the silver leaves, figures and greeting.

Above: A Wedding or Anniversary card using a medium & small flower

Above: An Anniversary card for a Silver Wedding

The Golden Wedding card is made with three small flowers, one medium and one large. All are made in a soft primrose colour of DMC Perlé with a pair of gold Twilley's Gold Dust along the outside edge. I cut a variety of leaves from gold paper-backed tinsel and marked on the veins with my thumb-nail, but it is much easier to buy gold leaves! As a finishing touch I added several gold flower-shaped sequins with a cup-shaped gold sequin on top.

These super cards are relatively quick to make and cost much less than a commercial greetings card — they're also much more fun to give and to receive. The cake decorating supplies offered in Newsagents or specialist shops provide you with a wealth of beautiful trimmings and neatly lettered messages. They might be intended for cake-decorating, but they are also perfect for card-decorating! Shop-bought leaves may not always be the right size for these small projects so you must be prepared to cut them down and re-shape them. This can be done by first cutting a smooth edged leaf of the required size, and then cutting new serrations letting the smooth shape dictate the finished outline as shown in the diagram.

Use the examples shown here to give you ideas of how to place your leaves and flowers to start with, you'll soon be making up your own arrangements and variations. However, let me give you one very vital word of warning — make absolutely sure that you have your card the right way round before you reach for the glue, it's only too easy to find that you have a beautiful card which opens backwards!

BIRTHDAY CARDS.

I made four small flowers and one large flower in shades of mauve and purple and mounted them on a dark green card 4¼" x 6" (10.5cm x 15cm) with an oval shaped cut out. The leaves are a white pearly-finished fabric type, but you could use silver leaves to match the silver-paper 'Happy Birthday' and the flower shaped silver sequin glued to the centre of the larger flower.

For a more ambitious Birthday or Best Wishes card use a larger card 5¼" x 6½" (13cm x 16cm) with a circular cut out and make one large, one medium and five small flowers, one of which is glued to the top of the largest flower. Use a variety of leaves and a commercially produced message.

As the ready-made artificial leaves may not be quite the right size for either of these projects you must be prepared to cut the leaves down in size and make a new serrated edge where necessary.

Left: A Golden Wedding card

Below: A simple Birthday card

Below: A more ambitious Best Wishes or Birthday card.

Above: How to make smaller leaves out of a larger one. First cut along the heavy lines, then if necessary trim to form a new serrated edge as shown on the left.

BIRTH CONGRATULATIONS CARD.

Use four small flowers and one medium sized flower in appropriate shades of blue or pink. Slip a toning piece of pink or blue card behind the oval cut out to form a background for the commercial 'Congratulations' and the silver stork. Two five-lobed leaves have been cut into smaller leaf shapes and one silver flower-shaped sequin has been glued into the centre of the medium sized flower.

4 small & 1 medium sized flower decorate a Birth Congratulations card

Pricking for daffodil trumpet

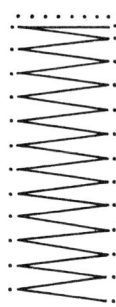

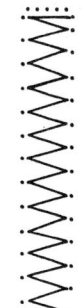

Pricking for narcissus trumpet

An Easter card made from a variety of yellow & orange coloured flowers

MORE COMPLEX FLOWERS.

To make an effective Easter card you will need two small flowers in gold and orange DMC Perlé, a narcissus in primrose yellow and orange and a daffodil made entirely in bright yellow.

The narcissus is made up of a medium size flower worked in half stitch. The centre is worked in four pairs of the same yellow passives, an orange worker and an outer pair of orange passives. The worker is twisted once between the yellow passives and the outer orange pair. On completing the strip, knot and trim off the passive pairs as usual. The longer worker thread is then used to stitch the overlap of the strip in place BEFORE running in the usual gathering thread, it is best if the neater, starting edge is the one on the inside surface of the flower centre. Pull the gathering thread up as tightly as possible, secure it with a double backstitch and trim off all the ends if you are intending to glue the centre onto the half stitch outer petals. It can be stitched in place if you prefer, but it is considerably more difficult to keep the trumpet in the centre as you sew.

The daffodil is made in bright yellow using a large sized flower made entirely in half stitch with 8 pairs. The trumpet is made in the same colour with 8 pairs of passives which need only be 12" (30cm) long and a worker (36" or 100cm long) which is only twisted at the end of each row. Again it is best to form the flower centre by stitching the overlap in place before adding the gathering thread. The centre is glued in place once the gathering thread has been pulled up tightly and the ends secured and removed.

Arrange your spring flowers around the cut out oval of a small card and glue each into place adding small green leaves as necessary. Your Easter Greeting can be a commercial paper one, or written inside the card using a gold or silver effect felt pen.

TORCHON TRIM FOR A HAIR SLIDE OR PONY TAIL BAND.

Using a very simple strip of torchon consisting only of fans and ground, you can make attractive hair slides and pony-tail bands.

1 pair of DMC 80 Cordonnet Special as workers. Cut 1 2 yard (2m) length.
1 pair of Twilley's Gold Dust, or a doubled length of fine metallic thread for the outside passive. Cut 1 24" (60cm) length.
5 pairs of DMC 80 Cordonnet Special as passives. Cut 5 1 yard (1m) lengths.
2 pairs of DMC 80 Cordonnet Special for inside passives. Cut 2 24" (60cm) lengths.

If you prefer to work the fans in half stitch instead of cloth stitch, cut 6 lengths of DMC 80 Cordonnet Special 55" (140cm) long instead of the workers and the five pairs of passives.

WORKING INSTRUCTIONS.

Hang the glittery pair of outside passives on pin 1 and push the bobbins to the left, hang the workers (or one pair of passives for the half stitch fan) around the same pin and put the bobbins down to the right of the previous pair. Now twist the middle two threads twice, then twist both pairs once (twist the worker pair once more if you are working cloth stitch fans). Hang one pair of passives on each of pins T1, T2 and T3. You can now complete the whole of the fan working either in cloth stitch or half stitch. Don't forget that if you are making half stitch fans you must make a double half stitch (or cloth stitch and twist) with the contrasting coloured edge pair each time, and if you are working cloth stitch fans, that you will need to twist the workers twice before cloth stitching through the glittery outside passive pair. In either variation you must twist the workers twice at the end of every row and to twist the three pairs coming out of each fan twice before taking them into the ground.

Hang a new pair of passives on T4 and work a torchon ground stitch (half stitch, pin, half stitch and twist) for pin 12 with the new pair and the pair which leaves the fan after pin 6. Remove pin T4 to allow the new pair to slide down and rest around pin 12. Hang the shortest inner passive pairs from pin 13 and cloth stitch the righthand pair from pin 12 through them, twist it twice (but don't twist the inner passive pairs at all). Hang the final passive pair from T5 and make a torchon ground stitch with the two righthand-most pairs at pin 14, remove T5 and tension carefully. Cloth stitch the lefthand pair from pin 14 through the inner passive and twist it twice. Complete the area of torchon ground before returning to the edge to work the next fan. (If you prefer you can work a proper footside down the straight edge as shown in the finished pieces on the right.)

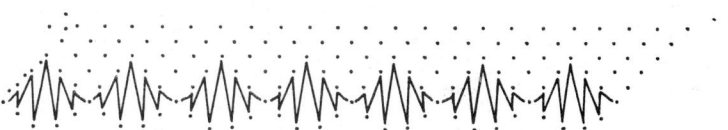

Pricking for the torchon trim

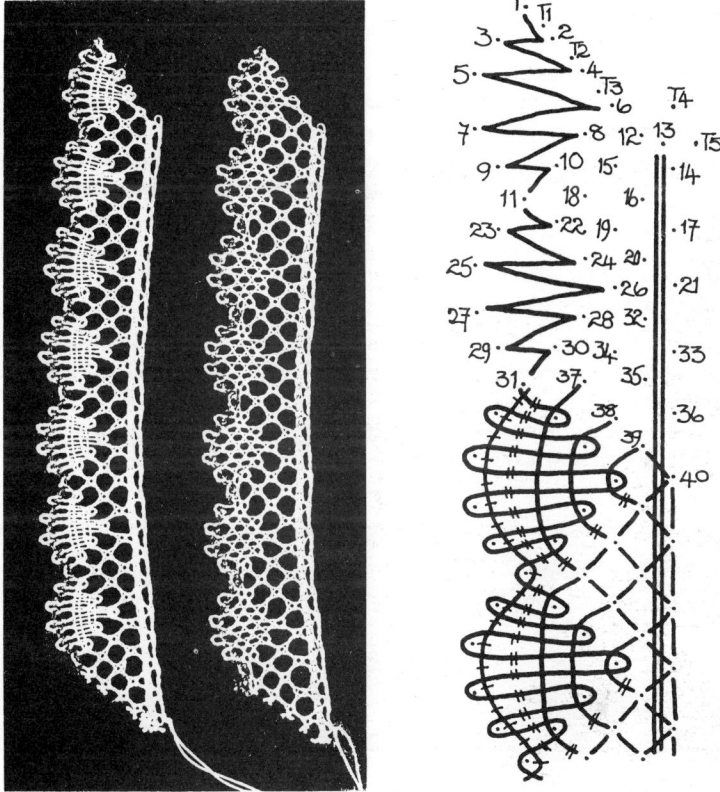

Above Left: Finished strips showing fans worked in half-stitch (right) & in cloth stitch (left)
Above Right: Working diagram for torchon strip with cloth stitch fans

Complete seven fans in this way and work the usual area of torchon ground afterwards, but add one extra row of ground which will give you an underlap to stitch to the very first diagonal row of pinholes which was completed at the start of the strip. Reef knot each pair of passives around the final pins, tie off the inner passives in the same way. Leave one pair of threads at the straight edge untrimmed and use them to stitch the overlap in place and then after securing it well with a double backstitch start the gathering thread which is run in through the pinholes along the straight edge. Pull it up, but do not pull it up to its fullest extent, allow it to form a larger circle in the centre so that the outer fans lie smoothly without being gathered into a frill. Fasten off well, but leave your sewing thread attached so that you can use it to attach the centre decoration and ribbon trim.

The ribbon trim is made up of very narrow satin ribbon ⅛" (3mm) in width. First of all tie a single knot at the end of the length trying not to twist the ribbon too much as the knot is pulled tight. Again, keeping the ribbon smooth, tie a second knot over the top of and around the first to enlarge it. Pull it as tight as you can and trim off the short piece of ribbon which may project from the centre of the knot. This can be trimmed off really close without any danger of the ribbon fraying because of the knot. Now thread two glass beads onto the long end of the ribbon, I used two 'knitting' beads which are about ¼" (5mm) in diameter and have quite a large hole. Push the beads right down to rest against the knots, and measure 8" (20cm) from the end and tie a second pair of knots, one on top of the other, at this point. Trim off the surplus ribbon and bring the second bead down to rest against the knot. Fold the ribbon in two so that one is about 1" (2.5cm) longer than the other and stitch it across the centre of the torchon trim.

The centre decoration can be made up of a small sized flower in DMC Perlé and Twilley's Gold Dust to match the outer passive in the piece of torchon, or you might like to make a small flower out of ten cup-shaped sequins and some small glass beads. Whichever you choose, stitch it to the centre of the torchon strip and then stitch everything to the end of the slide you have chosen to make a really attractive hair decoration. You can add another glass bead to the centre of the lace flower as a finishing touch.

Hair slide with sequin flower centre.

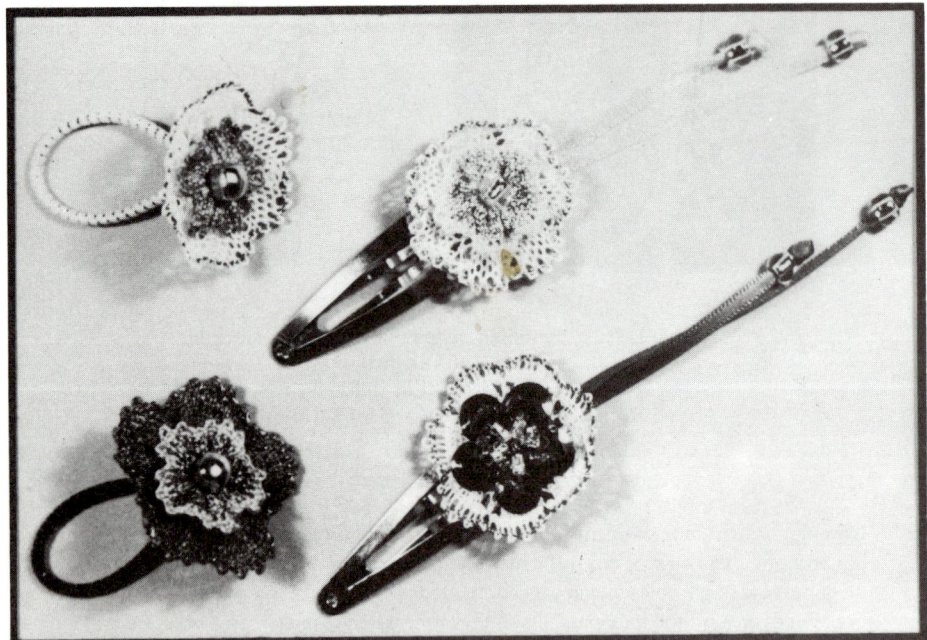

Top Left:	Pony-tail band with small flower in the centre of the torchon trim which has half-stitch fans.
Bottom Left:	Pony-tail band made up of one small & one large flower.
Top Right:	Hair slide with small flower and trim with half-stitch fans.
Bottom Right:	Hair slide with a small sequin flower & torchon trim with cloth stitch fans.

To use these decorations on a pony tail band you can assemble the same torchon lace trim and one small-sized flower. Make sure you have bought the pony-tail bands with a very large gold bead fastening the ends of the elastic together. (The gold bead must be larger than the hole in the middle of the small lace flower so that the flower cannot come off.) Pass the doubled elastic down through the centre of the small flower and then through the centre of the torchon trim (or indeed a large-sized flower worked in toning Perlé or Gold Dust). Push the decorations close up against the gold bead and it's ready for use. Because there is no need to stitch the two layers together it is easy to alter the combinations of trim and flowers to produce very different effects and colour schemes.

HEARTS FOR VALENTINES, WEDDINGS AND ANNIVERSARIES.

TINY TAPE LACE HEART.

This very small heart motif can be quickly made to decorate a small gift box or a gift tag. Worked in red it is ideal for Valentine's Day or birthdays, in white with silver or gold passives it is suitable for weddings or anniversaries.

2 pairs of Twilley's Gold Dust as passives. Cut 2 20" (50cm) lengths.
1 pair of DMC Coton Perlé as workers. Cut 1 60" (150cm) length.

WORKING INSTRUCTIONS.

Wind half the thread onto each bobbin as usual and hang the two glittery pairs on pins T1 and T2. The workers are hung from pin 3. The tape is worked in cloth stitch, with two twists on the workers at the end of every row. Tension the threads well at the end of each row to keep your trail flat and smooth. Press the pins down into the pillow as your heart progresses so that you are always working comfortably.

You will need to make several 'sewings' to link the trails together as you go round. The first sewing will be when you are just a little over half way through your heart, one worker thread will be pulled through the loop around pin 8 with a crochet hook to form a loop through which the other worker bobbin is then passed. Replace the pin taking care not to split any of the threads, and tension the workers carefully. Continue with your trail until you reach the V of the heart where the new part of the trail crosses over the top of the old. You will need to use three pinholes a second time here, but there is no need to make sewings into all of them. Make a sewing into just the last of the shared pinholes, and simply use the first and second pins again without removing them, slipping the worker behind each pin before continuing the trail. Make sure that you follow the zig-zag markings on the heart carefully at this point. Continue the trail, making a sewing just a few rows before the end. The final sewing comes at the point where the workers use pin 4 for the second time. Use pin 3 again too, but without doing a sewing, take the workers back to the inner edge and tie them in a reef knot at pin 4, knot off all the passives in the same way and trim the ends close to the knots. Remove your pins and turn the heart over. It can now be glued to a gift tag or the front of a gift box.

If a young child is attempting this piece you can reduce the number of sewings by omitting one at the crossing of the trails at the V as the heart should hold its shape without this and a spot of glue between the two trails will be effective once the piece is off the pillow. With care you can also avoid the final sewing at the join by simply using the pins again and making a small overlap before tying off all the ends. Again a spot of glue will keep the overlap in place more permanently.

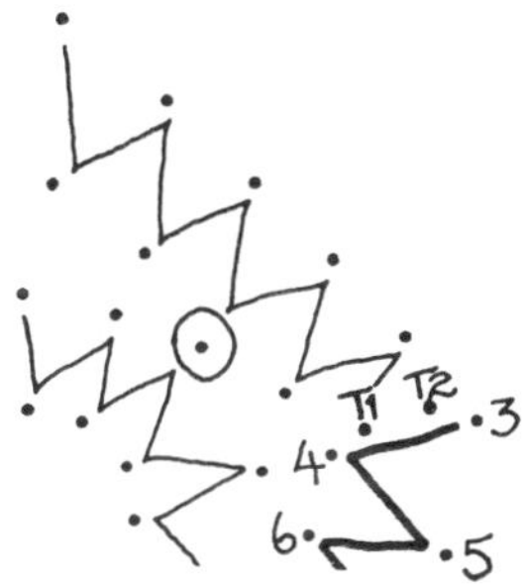

Above: Working diagram to start heart

Gift box decorated with small tape lace heart

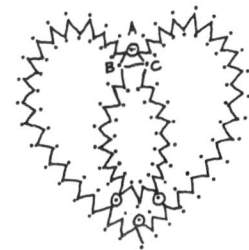

Left: Pricking for tape lace heart
Make sewings at circled pinholes

Below Left: Working through the V of the heart for the first time.
Below Right: Crossing the previous trail when working the V for the second time

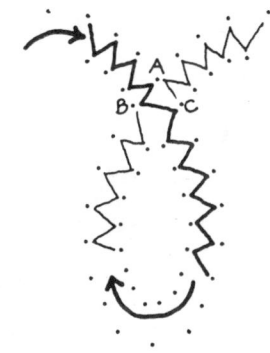 

LARGE TAPE LACE HEART.

3 pairs of Twilley's Gold Dust as passives. Cut 3 40" (100cm) lengths.
1 pair of DMC Coton Perlé as workers. Cut 1 110" (275cm) length.

This very simple heart shape is quite straightforward to work and makes a good Valentine project after Christmas if worked in red or gold passives with red workers.

WORKING INSTRUCTIONS.

Hang the passive pairs across the top of the trail and the workers at the righthand end. Work in cloth stitch twisting the workers twice at the end of every row. Make sure that you tension carefully to keep the surface of your trail nice and smooth.

Make a sewing when you come to pin 11 for the second time. You will also need to make a sewing where the trails cross at the V of the heart. There are three shared pinholes at this point and you can make a sewing into each, alternatively you can use the first and second shared pin in the usual way and make a sewing only at the third shared pinhole. Continue working the trail, making one more sewing into the circled pinhole towards the end of the piece. At the join make a sewing with your workers into pinholes 1 and 5, tie off the workers and then all three pairs of passives. Trim the ends close to the knots, remove the pins and turn the piece over to the right side.

This can be mounted onto the front of a simple card and your greeting written inside. I used a piece of card 7½" x 3¼" (18cm x 8.5cm) and folded it in half.

Pricking for large tape lace heart

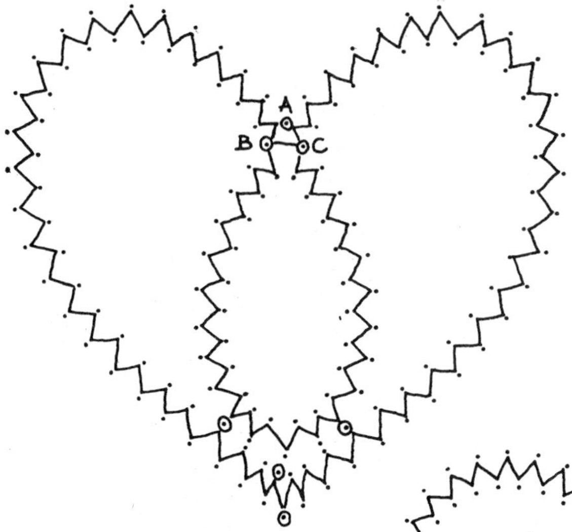

Above: Finished tape lace heart

Right: Pricking for heart with raised chain

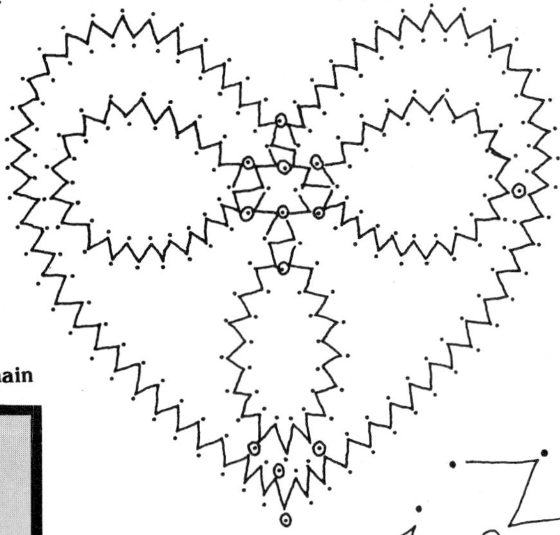

Right: Diagram showing how to work through the V of the heart for the first time

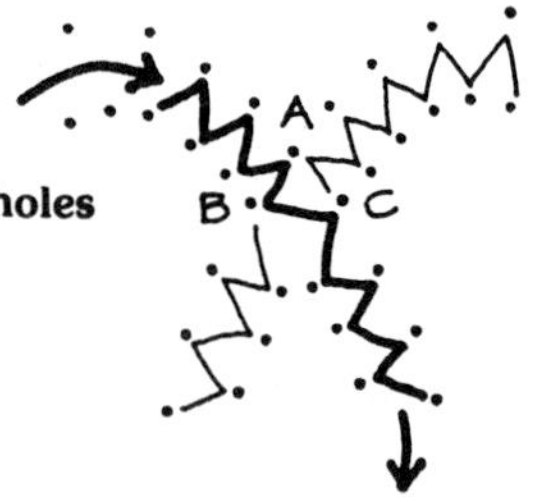

Below Right: Working through the V of the heart for the second time. Make sewings into circled pinholes

Below: Finished heart with raised chain

Below: Working diagram for start of large tape lace heart.

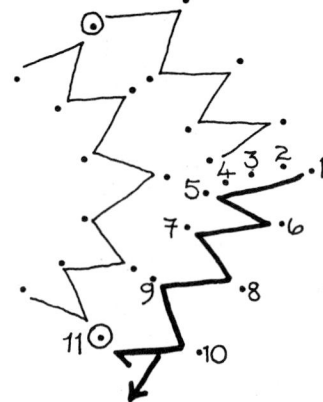

Right: Working diagram for the start of the heart with raised chain

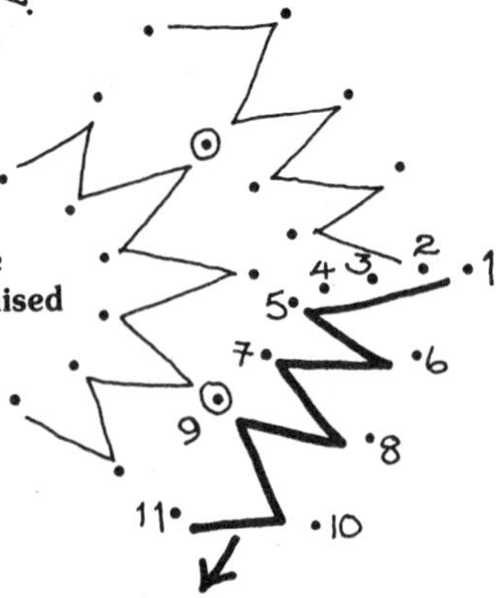

HEART WITH RAISED CHAIN.

4 pairs of DMC Fil a Dentelle as side passives. Cut 4 60" (150cm) lengths.
1 pair of DMC Fil a Dentelle as workers. Cut 1 150" (375cm) length.
2 pairs of Twilley's Gold Dust as chain passives. Cut 2 72" (180cm) lengths.

This is a more challenging project than the two previous hearts and is suitable for older or more skilful children.

WORKING INSTRUCTIONS.

On the three temporary pins across the top of the trail hang the gold passives astride the centre pin and two red passives in order on each of the two side pins. Hang the workers from the pin at the right of the trail. Cloth stitch the workers through the first two pairs of red passives, now pick up the two worker bobbins together and pass them under the first gold thread, over the two centre ones and underneath the gold thread on the left, now cloth stitch them through the two pairs of red passives to the left in the usual way and twist them twice before putting up the pin at the end of row. Tension all the threads before lifting the two outside gold threads up and over the two centre threads, bringing them towards each other and putting them down side by side between the two other gold threads. (So you have in fact twisted the righthand pair of gold threads in the usual way right over left, but you have twisted the lefthand gold pair left over right.) You are now ready to work the next row.

Cloth stitch through the first two red passive pairs, then pass the workers together (as if they were one thread) under the first gold thread, over the centre two and under the righthand gold thread, now complete the row cloth stitching through the passives as normal. Change the positions of the gold threads, bringing the outside two threads into the middle. This makes a very fine chain-stitch effect along the top of your trail.

The heart is worked as a tape, with several sewings linking adjacent trails as the work progresses. I have circled those pinholes where sewings are necessary on the pricking, where the trails cross over each other there are four shared pinholes each time, I suggest that you make a sewing into the first and last of each group of four, using the other two pins for a second time in the usual way. Make a sewing at each end of the row to overlap the starting line, cloth stitch the workers back to the inside edge and make a reef knot, tie a reef knot with each of the red passives, and tie off the gold threads. Trim the ends close to the knots, remove the pins and your heart is ready to mount on a simple card sized 7½" x 3½" (18cm x 8.5cm).

⟵ Direction of Working

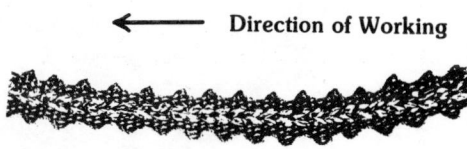

Sample showing the raised chain effect

DOUBLE LAYER HEART.

The larger heart shape is worked in half stitch using all red threads for a Valentine, or with blue threads for a wedding or anniversary card. The slightly smaller white and gold heart is a simple torchon edging worked entirely in cloth stitch fans and torchon ground.

6 pairs of DMC Fil a Dentelle. Cut 6 72" (180cm) lengths.
1 pair of Twilley's Gold Dust as outer passives in a colour to match the finer passives. Cut 1 40" (100cm) length.

WORKING INSTRUCTIONS FOR LOWER HALF STITCH HEART.

Hang one pair of fine threads on the pin at the deepest point of the V, hang two pairs on the next pin to its left, one more pair on each of the next three pins and the pair of glittery threads on the next. Start with the righthand-most pair as your workers and half stitch across to the left through the pairs hanging on that pin, twist the workers twice, remove the pin and put it up again in the same pinhole between the workers and the other two pairs. Work back in half stitch and twist twice before putting up the pin, tension the threads and work back taking in a new pair before taking out the pin (from which the new pair is hanging) and putting it up again in the same hole. Keep working in this way until you reach the glittery thread hanging from the lefthand pin. You must remember to make a double half stitch (cloth stitch and twist) everytime you come to this pair so that it stays as the outlining thread around the scalloped edge. Twist the worker twice at each end of the row as usual.

Continue working taking care to tension well at the end of every row. Make sure that the outside glittery pair of passives stays in its correct position and that you keep the workers in step with the zig zag pathway marked on the pricking, the pinholes are quite close together along the inner edge of the curve and it is only too easy to miss one.

At the end of the piece sew the worker pair into each of the pinholes shared with the starting rows, leaving one pair of passives out after each sewing (ie. make the sewing, work back to the inner edge of the border and work back through all but the last passive pair to make the next sewing.) These passive pairs can be reef-knotted and cut off at the end. You will have two pairs at the last pin hole which can be knotted together. Make the ending as neat as you can, but remember that the whole of this join will be covered by the white piece which will go on top!

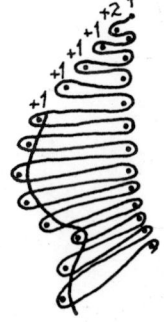

Diagram showing the start of the half-stitch lower-layer heart

23

Above: Pricking for half-stitch lower-layer heart

Above & Below: Finished lace hearts

Above: Working diagram for top layer heart

Below: Pricking for torchon top-layer heart

Below: Finished card with the two layers in place

DOUBLE LAYER HEART (Contd.)

4 pairs of DMC 80 Cordonnet Special as passives. Cut 4 48" (120cm) lengths.
1 pair of DMC 80 Cordonnet Special as workers. Cut 1 4 yard (4m) length.
2 pairs of Mez Effektgarn or similar fine metal thread as passives. Cut 2 30" (75cm) lengths.

WORKING INSTRUCTIONS FOR TOP HEART.

Hang one pair of white workers from pin 1 and push it to the left, hang one pair of white passives from the same pin and put them down to the right of the first pair. Twist the centre two threads twice, and then twist each pair twice more. Hang a gold passive pair from pin 2 and cloth stitch the worker through it twisting the worker twice and the gold pair once. Hang one pair of white passives from each of pins T1, T2 and T3. Using the worker and each new pair in turn work a torchon ground stitch (half stitch, pin, half stitch and twist) putting up pins 3, 4 and 5. Remove pins T1, T2 and T3 and let the new pairs slide down to rest snugly around pins 3, 4 and 5. Hang the gold passive from pin 6 and cloth stitch the workers through it, twist the workers twice and gold pair once, put up pin 7 at the start of the fan.

Now go back to the inner edge and complete the area of ground. Cloth stitch the pair from pin 3 through the gold passive (always twist the gold passive once and the white thread twice) to make a ground stitch with the pair from pin 1 at pin 8, take the lefthand of these pairs back through the gold passive and again twist the white thread twice and the gold pair once. Now complete the row of torchon ground pins 9 and 10. Using the pair from pin 9 make up the straight edge at pin 11 and make a ground stitch at pin 12. Make up the edge pin 13. You are now ready to go back and work the fan.

Cloth stitch the workers back through the gold outside passives, twisting the passives once and the worker twice, cloth stitch through the incoming ground pair at pin 14, twist the workers twice, tension the threads and work back to the outside remembering to twist both the workers and the outside passives as necessary. Complete the fan remembering to take in a new pair at the righthand end of each row for as long as the fan continues to get wider and leaving out a pair of passives as it gets narrower. This will bring you to pin 23. Twist each of the three pairs of passives coming out of the fan at pins 18, 20 and 22 twice, you are now ready to start the next area of ground.

Continue working until you have completed the final fan and the last triangle of torchon ground. The worker and the outside gold passive are joined into pinhole 7, one white passive pair will be sewn into each of pinholes 5, 4 and 3, the gold inside passive into pinhole 2 and the final white passive into pin 1. Tie each pair securely with a reef knot and trim the ends close to the knot.

A piece of bright green card 4⅛" x 3⅞" (10.5cm x 9.75cm) folded in half provides a strong background colour for a red heart, a pale blue card would be better for a wedding. Glue the half stitch heart into place, then put the white heart edging on top, using a very thin line of glue along the straight inner edge and a spot of glue under each fan. A small embroidered flower motif to match the colour of the half stitch heart completes the piece.

HEART EDGING WITH A HEART—SHAPED FAN

I chose to work this edging in two colours — red and white. The red workers and outside passives give the appearance of a red heart-shaped fan contrasting nicely with the white torchon ground. The pinholes are quite close together in places, so it is a piece more suitable for an experienced child.

5 pairs of DMC 80 Cordonnet Special as passives. Cut 5 48" (120cm) lengths.
1 pair of DMC Fil a Dentelle as workers. Cut 1 5yd (5m) length.
1 pair of DMC Fil a Dentelle as outer passives. Cut 1 40" (100cm) length.

Left: Finished lace

Right: Pricking for heart edging with heart-shaped fan.

WORKING INSTRUCTIONS.

Hang the red workers on pin 1 and push them to the left, hang one pair of white passives from the same pin putting the bobbins down to the right of the previous pair. Twist the centre two threads twice and then each pair of bobbins twice more. Hang one pair of white passives from each of pins T1, T2, T3 and T4. With the red worker pair and one new pair in turn, work torchon ground stitches (half stitch, pin, half stitch and twist) at each of pins 2, 3, 4 and 5. Now remove the four temporary pins and let the new threads slide down to hang around the permanent pins. Hang the red passive from pin 6 and cloth stitch the red workers through it, twist the outside passive once and the workers twice before putting up pin 7 at the start of the fan.

Now return to the inside area of ground. Take the pair from pin 2 and make a ground stitch at pin 8 with the pair from pin 1, complete the diagonal row of ground pins at 9, 10 and 11. Go back to the edge and make up the next row of ground at pins 12, 13, and 14. Then work torchon ground stitches at pins 15, 16, and 17. You are now ready to work the fan.

Taking the worker from pin 7 cloth stitch it through the outside passive twisting the passive once and the worker twice, cloth stitch through the incoming ground pair and twist the worker twice before putting up pin 18, complete the fan in the usual way which will bring you to pin 31. Don't forget to twist the pairs coming out of the fan at pins 24, 26, 28 and 30. Now you are ready to work the next triangle of ground.

Above: Templates for heart-shape cut-outs.
  Larger - for card background glued to inside of card.
  Smaller - for cut-out in front of card

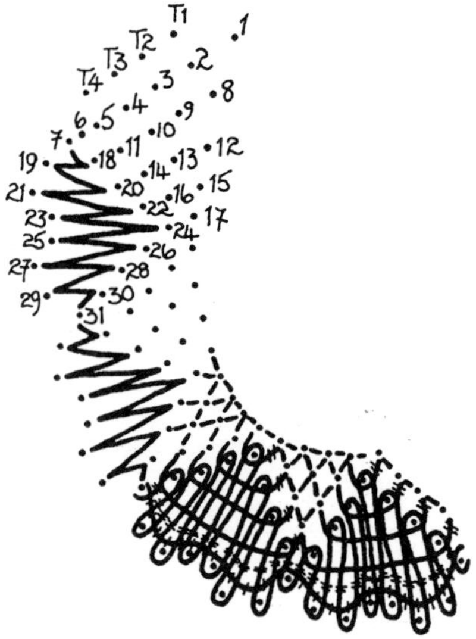

Finished card showing heart-shaped cut out & ribbon bow trimming

Left: Working diagram for Heart Edging with Heart-Shaped Fan.

At the end you will find that the red worker and outside passive both sew into pin 7, and the five white passives into pins 5, 4, 3, 2, and 1. Tie a reef knot at each pin and trim off close to the knots.

I mounted this heart-shaped piece on a larger green card heart and glued it to the inside of a cream card with a slightly smaller heart-shaped cut out on the front. A white ribbon bow can be added if you wish.

WEDDING HORSESHOES

I have designed two horseshoes, one is a large horseshoe intended to be carried by a bride, and the other is a much smaller and simpler version which could decorate the front of a wedding or anniversary card.

A WEDDING OR ANNIVERSARY CARD

Most of this horseshoe is made in half stitch with a double half stitch at each edge so that two blue passive pairs form the outline. It is decorated with two small blue flowers and two silver leaves which match the commercial 'Best Wishes'.

6 pairs of Twilley's Gold Dust in silver. Cut 6 2 yd (2m) lengths.
2 pairs of DMC Coton Perlé No 8 in blue. Cut 2 36" (90cm) lengths.

WORKING INSTRUCTIONS.

Wind half of each length of thread onto each bobbin as usual. Hang blue pairs on pin 1 and pin 5, one silver pair on each of pins 6 and 3, and two pairs of silver threads on each of pins 2 and 4. Hang these double pairs on 'in order', ie. hang one pair around the pin and push both of these bobbins to one side, hang the second pair around the pin and put both bobbins down EITHER to the left of the previous pair, OR to their right.

Taking the pair from pin 6 as your workers cloth stitch through all the passives twisting the workers twice at the end of every row. Work four rows in this way tensioning all the threads carefully. Leaving the workers around the pin at the end of the fourth row twist every pair of passives, both silver and blue, once. Work four more rows of cloth stitch, then again twist every passive pair once. Now change to half stitch working a double half stitch (or cloth stitch and twist) every time you come to the blue passives to ensure that they stay at the edge. Continue to twist the workers twice at the end of each row.

Continue in half stitch in this way until you reach the other end of the horseshoe. Once you reach pin A change to cloth stitch and work four rows, then twist all the passives once and work four more rows of cloth stitch. Now tie off the workers with a reef knot around the final pin and tie a reef knot with each of the passive pairs before trimming the threads close to the knots. Remove the pins and turn under the first four rows of cloth stitch along the 'fold-line' created by the row of twists. Glue this in place using Bostik. Do exactly the same at the finishing end so that all your knots are hidden behind the work. Your horseshoe is now ready to mount.

You will need a large card 5¼" x 6½" (13.5cm x 16.5cm) with a circular cut out. Slip a piece of blue card behind the cut out and glue the horseshoe into place paying special attention to the double thickness at each end. Now work two small blue flowers using the smallest size pattern in the flower section. I made one with 3 pale blue inner passives, a darker blue worker and outside passive, and the other entirely in pale blue. These are glued to the horseshoe, slightly overlapping one above the other. Tuck two small silver leaves underneath one flower and glue a silver 'Best Wishes' inside the horseshoe to complete the card.

Left: Pricking for a small horseshoe

Below: Finished card showing horseshoe decorated with 2 small flowers

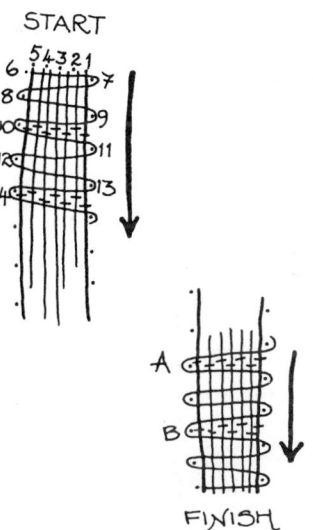

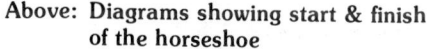

Above: Diagrams showing start & finish of the horseshoe

A BRIDE'S HORSESHOE

The majority of this horseshoe is made in honeycomb stitch ie. half stitch twist, pin, half stitch and twist, but there is no reason why it should not be worked in basic torchon ground with honeycomb diamonds. It is worked in silver with a blue outlining thread at each side. I chose to decorate it with silk flowers, but you could work a group of flowers similar to those used on the Alice band if you prefer.

8 pairs of Twilley's Gold Dust in silver. Cut 8 4yd (4m) lengths.
2 pairs of DMC Coton Perlé No 8 in blue. Cut 2 48" (120cm) lengths.

WORKING INSTRUCTIONS

Hang one blue pair on each of pins 1 and 7. Hang one silver pair on each of pins 2, 4, 6 and 8. Hang two pairs of silver threads 'in order' from pins 3 and 5. The pair at pin 8 will start out as your worker. Cloth stitch the first 6 rows putting two twists on the workers at the end of every row and tensioning the passives carefully to keep the work smooth. Leaving the workers at the end of the sixth row put one twist on all the passives, both blue and silver. Continue to work in cloth stitch until you reach pin A.

Twist the blue passive closest to pin A once and the worker twice, then cloth stitch back through the blue passive twisting it once more and the silver threads twice. Take the righthand-most silver thread and cloth stitch it to its right through the blue edge passive, twist it twice and the blue pair once and put up pin E, work the silver pair back through the blue passives and again twist the blue pair once and the silver pair twice.

You will find 6 silver pairs coming out of the cloth stitch between pins A and E, so take the lefthand two pairs and work a honeycomb stitch (half stitch and twist) above and below pin B, use the two centre pairs to work pin C and the two righthand pairs for pin D.

Continue working using honeycomb stitches for all the inside pins, and at the edge simply cloth stitching the silver pair through the blue pair, twisting the worker twice and the blue passive once before cloth stitching the silver pair back through the blue passive twisting the blue threads once and silver threads twice. Follow the markings on the pattern to work honeycomb diamonds as the horseshoe gets wider.

Put up the final row of honeycomb pins in the usual way and then using the silver pair from the lefthand edge of the work as your workers, cloth stitch seven rows. Put one twist on each of the passives and work six more rows of cloth stitch. Make a reef knot with the worker threads around the final pin and then tie off each pair of passives with a reef knot. Trim all the ends close to the knots and remove the pins.

Fold over the ends of the horseshoe along the 'foldline' of twists six rows in from both the start and the finish. Glue or stitch through the two layers to keep the underlap firmly in place and all the knots hidden from view. Cut a piece of 3/8-1/2" (1cm) wide white ribbon approximately 10" (25cm) long, more if you wish. Stitch the ribbon firmly through both thicknesses of the underlap to make a carrying loop.

You will need to cut a double thickness of stiff white card to form the base of your horseshoe. Placing your lace on the top surface of card draw lightly round the edge of the lace in pencil. Cut out the horseshoe cutting 1/16" (1mm) or so inside the pencil line so that the edges of the card will be completely hidden by the edge of the lace. Cut out two pieces of card and glue them together. Using the glue as sparingly as you can glue the lace to the card background and add the arrangement of silk flowers if you wish. The two small flowers at the ends of the horseshoe not only add some welcome decoration, but they also hide any problems you might have had in changing from cloth stitch to honeycomb ground and vice versa!

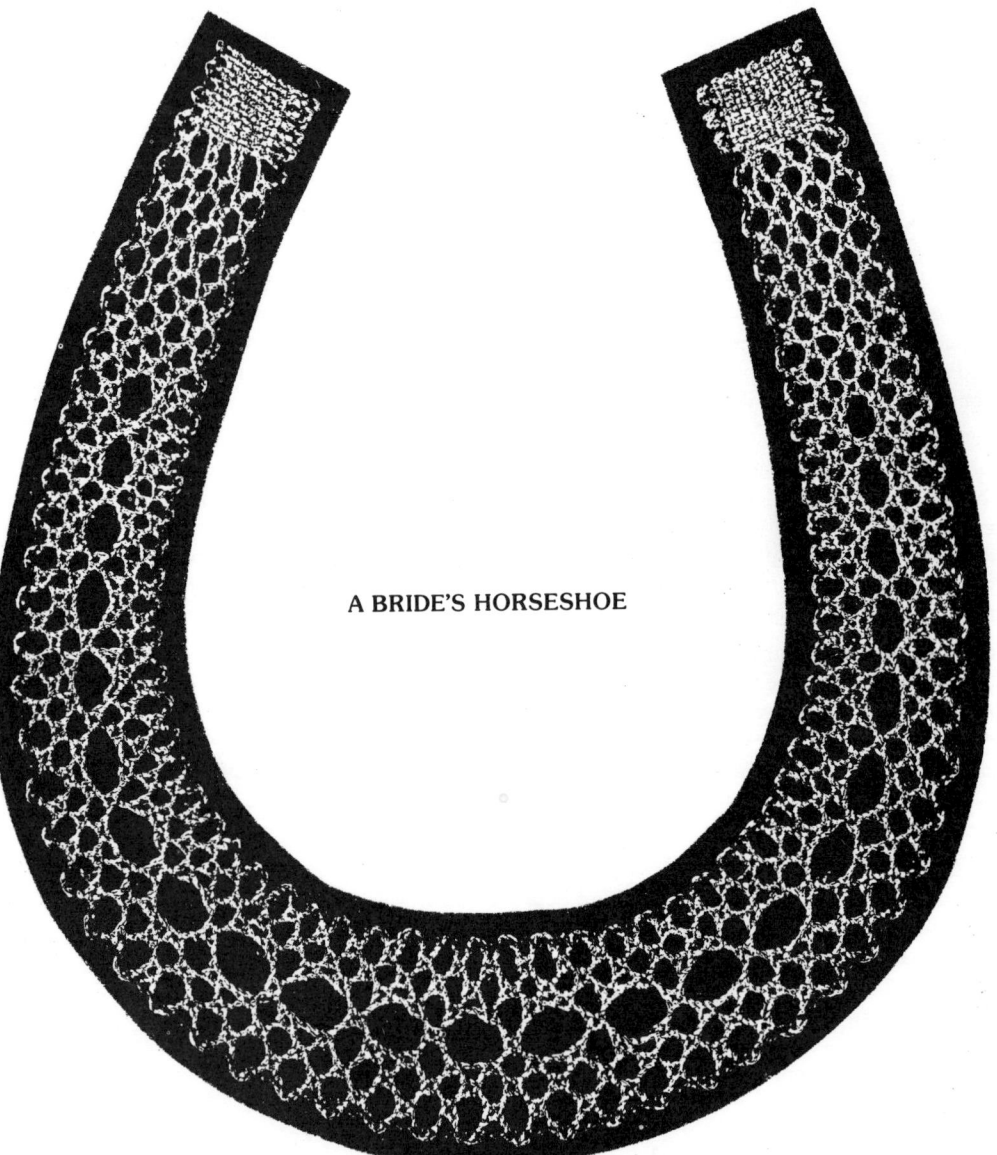

A BRIDE'S HORSESHOE

If you wish you could make a second piece of lace and glue it to the back of the horseshoe, or you could use a silver-effect felt pen to write on the bride and groom's names and wedding date.

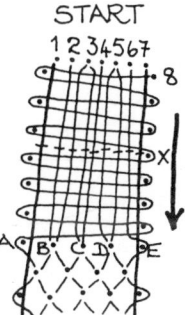
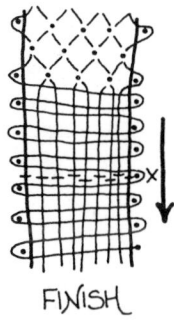

Above: Diagrams showing the start & finish of the large horseshoe

Below: Finished horseshoe

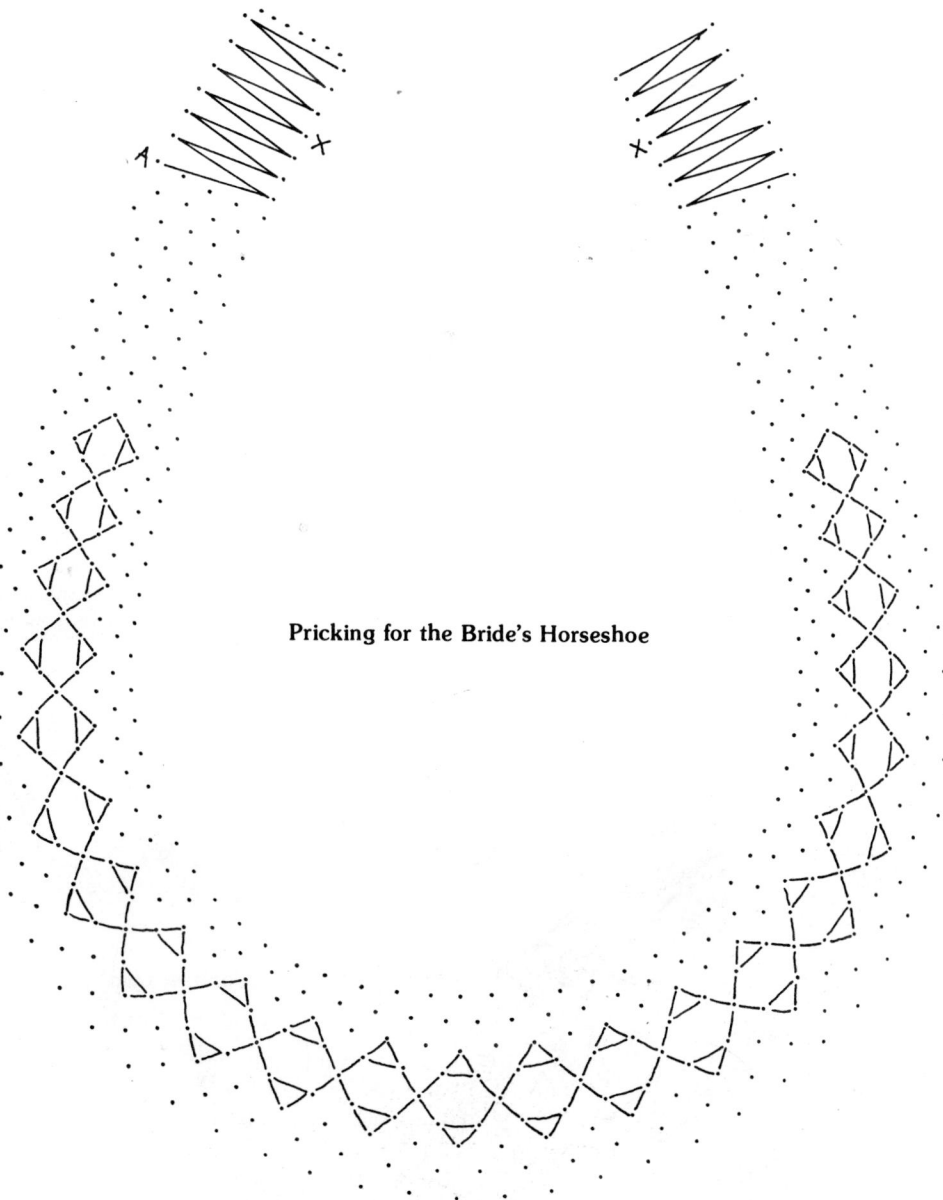

Pricking for the Bride's Horseshoe

HAIRBANDS

Here are two simple patterns which a child can use to make hairbands. Both are based on two cloth stitch trails which cross through each other to give a chain-like effect. One is simply stitched down onto a piece of corded ribbon, and the other has ribbon slotted through it. Both look very eyecatching when worked with glittery thread.

HAIRBAND 1

2 pairs of DMC Coton Perlé No 8 as workers. Cut 2 144" (360m) lengths.
4 pairs of Twilley's Gold Dust as passives. Cut 4 50" (125cm) lengths.

WORKING INSTRUCTIONS

It may help a young lacemaker to make a good job of the crossings if you select two pairs of dark coloured bobbins for the passives of one trail and two pairs of light coloured bobbins for the other trail. Hang one pair of glittery passives from each of pins 1, 2, 3 and 4, (the dark bobbins from pins 1 and 2, and the lighter ones from pins 3 and 4). Now you are ready to make your first trail crossing and if it is correctly completed the dark bobbins will end up as passives for the trail on the right of the work and the light coloured ones the trail on the left.

To work the crossing take the middle two pairs and cloth stitch them together, make a cloth stitch with the two lefthand pairs and then the two righthand pairs, finally make a cloth stitch with the two centre pairs.

Now hang the worker pairs on pins 5 and 6 and you are ready to start the trails. Cloth stitch through the passives and put two twists on the workers at the end of each row before putting up the pin. Make sure that the work is tensioned well at the end of every row so that the trails lie smooth and flat. Work both trails until you come to pin A on each side — twist the workers twice and put up the pins as usual. Now you need to work a 'kiss' stitch which is simply a cloth stitch and two more twists, this makes the workers change sides and work through the opposite trail to pin B where they are twisted twice in the usual way. After putting up pin B they work inwards towards the centre where they are twisted twice as usual before putting up pin C. The second 'kiss' is now made by just cloth stitching the workers together and twisting them twice before continuing the trail, remembering that the worker that was briefly on the righthand trail will now be on the left and vice versa.

Because there are two kiss stitches in quick succession the workers will in fact work only one pin on the opposite trail before returning to their more usual side. Make sure that you follow the markings on the pattern accurately, the pathways of the workers are clearly marked. Also remember to twist both workers twice BEFORE and AFTER the cloth stitch of the kiss before continuing with the trail. The other possible error is to to be so concerned with the 'kiss' stitch that you completely forget to put up pins A or C before making the cloth stitch of the kiss.

Work both trails down to pin D, the workers will now wait whilst the four passives of the trails cross through each other. This is done with four cloth stitches as described at the start of the piece. It can also be thought of as the first half of a spider. Once the crossing is completed the trails are continued, taking great care not to miss either of the two pinholes which are positioned quite close together in the centre of the work just below the crossing.

You will need to make at least 14 'chains' to make a hairband long enough for a child, but the length can easily be adjusted by working more repeats if necessary. It is almost certain that you will need to move the lace up the pattern if it is to be worked comfortably by a child on the average 16/18" pillow. To do this you must wrap the bobbins securely in a cover cloth whilst you remove all the pins so that you can move the lace higher up the pattern to give you more working room again. To help you keep the bobbins in order you can use a length of ribbon threaded through the spangles with the ends tied together in a bow, or you could simply thread a knitting stitch-holder through each spangle and close it so that when you unwrap the cover cloth the bobbins can be slipped off either ribbon or stitch-holder in the correct order.

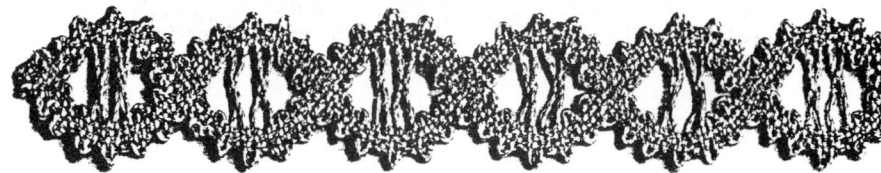

Above: Sample of finished lace

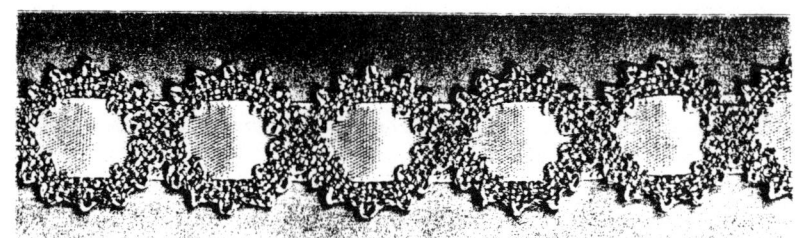

Above: Finished hairband showing ribbon threaded through

Below: Pricking for Hairband 1

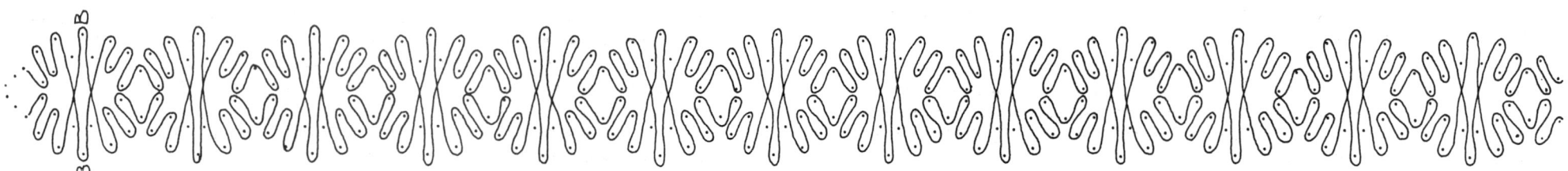

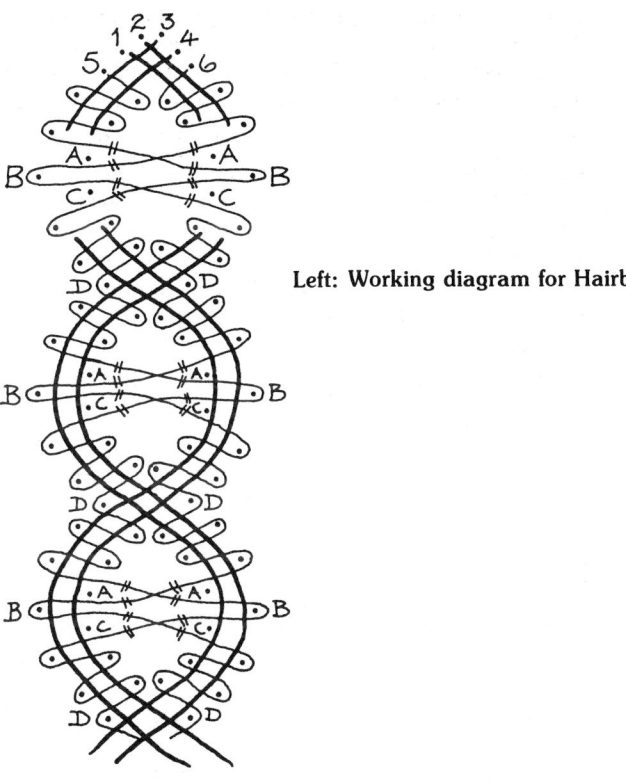

Left: Working diagram for Hairband 1

Hairband 1

Don't forget that when all the pins have been removed your work is very vulnerable and it is essential not to pull on any of the bobbins whilst your lace is unsecured. To help you avoid putting any tension on the threads, slope the pillow backwards as you take out the last few pins so that should your bundle of bobbins slip at all they will slip towards the work and not away from it. You can also put a couple of pins through the top or sides of the cover cloth to prevent it slipping at all. Always take out the pins from the back of the work first leaving the most recent pins in place until the last possible moment. Once the lace is free of all your pins, ease the lace and the bundle of bobbins back until the last two or three 'chains' which you worked are lying exactly over the first two or three marked on the pattern. Now replace all the pins in those repeats. Only when those pins are in place is it safe to gently open the cover cloth and remove the ribbon or stitch-holder so that the work can continue. For the young lacemaker moving up a piece of lace can be a worry, so a more experienced helping hand is usually very much appreciated.

Complete the final crossing and work two or three more pins on each trail. Tie the workers off with a reef knot around the last pin and then make a reef knot with each pair of passives. Trim off the ends close to the knots. These small sections of trail will be folded back underneath the last crossing so that all the knots will be well hidden. With a needle and thread stitch the underlaps in place.

Take a piece of 3/8" (1cm) wide ribbon approximately 12" (30cm) long, and thread it through the lace pushing it up immediately after the first crossing, taking it over the two kisses and then down underneath the next crossing. The kisses will be completely hidden by the ribbon. Neaten the end of the ribbon with a double hem and securely attach one end to a piece of 3/16" (5mm) wide elastic. Stitch the ribbon to the start of the lace. Now try the hairband on the child and measure the length of elastic you need to provide a good fit — probably somewhere in the region of 9" (22.5cm). Attach the elastic to the ribbon, neatening the ribbon with a double hem as before.

HAIRBAND 2

2 pairs of DMC Coton Perlé No 8 as workers. Cut 2 120" (300m) lengths.
4 pairs of Twilley's Gold Dust as 'chain' passives. Cut 4 48" (120cm) lengths.
2 pairs of Twilley's Gold Dust as straight edge passives. Cut 2 30" (75cm) lengths.

WORKING INSTRUCTIONS

It may help the lacemaker to work the crossings more easily if two of the 'chain' passives are wound onto light coloured bobbins and two onto darker bobbins. Hang two matching passives onto pins 1 and 2, and the other two pairs onto pins 3 and 4. You will now make four cloth stitches with these pairs to make a crossing. Take the centre two pairs and make the first cloth stitch, now do the same with the two righthand pairs, and then the two lefthand pairs. Finally make a cloth stitch with the two centre pairs again and you will find that the dark bobbins which may have started on the right will now be ready to work the trail on the left, and the light bobbins will have done the opposite.

To start the straight sides of the hairband hang the two Perlé worker pairs on pins 7 and 8, and the two glittery passive pairs on pins 5 and 6. Cloth stitch the workers through the passive pair and twist them twice. The glittery passive pair will remain untwisted throughout. Now cloth stitch the worker through the two passive pairs of the chain and twisting the workers twice put up the pin. Work back through the chain passives and twist the workers twice before cloth stitching through the edge passive. Twist the workers twice before putting up the edge pin. Cloth stitch back through the passive pair and this time only twist the workers once before working through the two chain passives, twisting twice and putting up the pin. Work back through the passives, twist the workers once, cloth stitch through the edge passive and twist twice before putting up the next edge pin. Cloth stitch the workers back into the centre and out again twisting them twice between the edge pair and the chain passives. Leave them at the outer edge pin A and work the second side of the chain until that worker too reaches pin A.

Now work a crossing with the four glittery chain passives using the four cloth stitches which you used to start the piece. The light and dark bobbins will now have changed sides again, and you are ready to work down one side and then the other until you reach the next crossing.

Continue in this way until you have worked sufficient length, moving the piece up the pillow if necessary. At the end work the final crossing, and bring the workers back into the centre to work the first pinhole as usual. Now work them back through only the chain passives before twisting twice and putting up a new pin just to the outside of the trail passives, work back to the centre of the chain, put in a new pin on the inside of the trail passives and tie a reef knot with the workers around it, putting an extra twist on the first half of the knot so that it will not slip before you can tie the second half. Work the second half of the chain in exactly the same way and finish it with reef knots. The outside edge passives can also be knotted, but don't trim them off short as they can later be threaded through to the wrong side of the corded ribbon which will form the backing for the hairband, tied together and cut off.

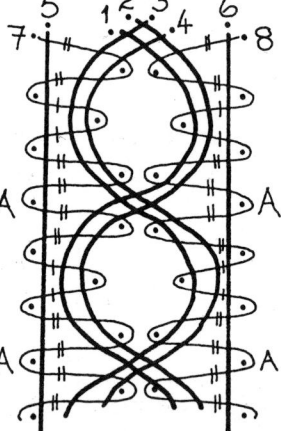

Right: Working Diagram for Hairband 2

Below: Finished Hairband with lace mounted onto ribbon

Above: Sample of finished lace   Below: Pricking for Hairband 2

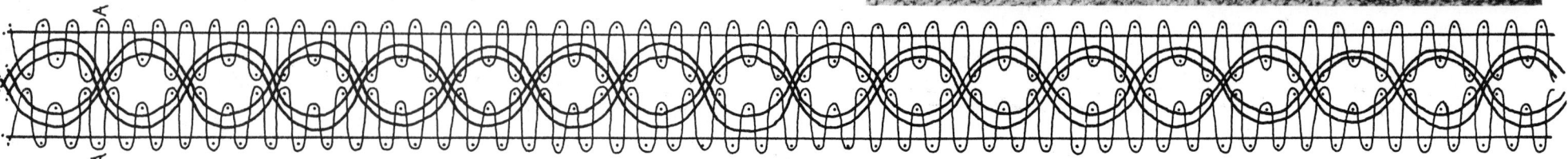

Use a piece of corded ribbon a little wider than the lace ¾" or 2.25cm, and about 12" (30cm) long. Make a double hem on one end and attach the elastic 3/16" (3mm) sewing it securely to the centre of the neatened edge, a 9" (24cm) length should be sufficient.

Now, take the neater, starting end of your lace and stitch it down onto the ribbon using a sewing thread which matches the colour of your lace. Work down first one straight side and fasten off before restarting once more at the neatened end and stitching the second straight side in place. Trim the ribbon to length allowing sufficient for another double hem. Stitch the finishing ends of the edge passives through the ribbon and fasten them off, then tuck the short sections of trail worked after the final crossing underneath that same crossing so that all the knots are well hidden. Stitch in place through all the thicknesses. Make the double hem to neaten the ribbon and attach the elastic making sure that it is not twisted.

Hairband 2

PROJECTS USING SIMPLE FLOWERS

CANDLE FLOUNCE

This straightforward piece of torchon makes a beautiful frill to go underneath a candle ring. By working one and a half times round the circular pattern and then mounting the lace on a backing of a larger diameter a gentle flounced effect is achieved, showing off the pattern in a way which gathers would otherwise have obscured. Because it is not essential to fix the frill to any one particular candle ring you can use the same piece of lace to go under any ring enabling you to vary the arrangement or colour scheme with the minimum of effort.

1 pair of Mez Effektgarn as inner footside passives. Cut 1 2yd (2m) length.
1 pair of Mez Effektgarn as outer passives. Cut 1 5yd (5m) length and use it double giving you 1¼yd (1.25cm) on each bobbin of the pair.
11 pairs of 36/2 Brok as passives. Cut 11 3yd (3m) lengths.
3 pairs of 36/2 Brok as workers. Cut 3 6yd (6m) lengths. You will need 1 pair of workers for the fan, and two pairs for the cloth stitch heart as each will be the worker on alternate hearts (remaining as the central passive when it is not the worker).

Finished candle flounce with floral candle ring in place

WORKING INSTRUCTIONS

Take the gold outside passive and hang it on pin 1, push the bobbins to the left. Take one of the white worker pairs and hang it round the same pin, put the bobbins down to the right of the previous pair and twist the centre two bobbins twice (right over left as usual). Now twist the gold passive pair once and the worker twice.

Hang three white passive pairs from pins T1, T2 and T3. You can now work the fan remembering always to twist the gold passive pair once and the worker twice both between the gold and white passives and at the end of every row. You must also remove each Temporary pin (T1, T2 & T3) two rows after each new pair has been taken into the work, tension the passives carefully so that they slide right down to rest on the workers. Now twist each of the passive pairs twice as they leave the fan (from pins 6, 8 and 10).

Start the heart by hanging the two white worker pairs from pin 12, push the first pair to the left, place the second pair to the right and twist the centre two threads twice. The righthand pair will be your workers for this repeat, working first towards the right to pin 13. Hang white passive pairs on pins T4-9 inclusive. Work the heart in cloth stitch tensioning the work well as you go as the cloth stitch is dense and you must make sure that everything is smooth before going on to the next row. Having completed the first half of the heart you must work the second fan before finishing the heart. Then twist all the passives leaving the heart twice.

Hang a white pair of passives from T10 and work a torchon ground stitch with the pair from the tip of the heart (pin 23) and put up pin 46, remove T10 and slide the new pair down to rest around pin 46. Put T10 back in place and hang the gold inner passive and the final white passive from it. Take the righthand pair from pin 46 and cloth stitch it through the gold pair, twist the gold pair once and the white pair twice. Now make a torchon ground stitch with the two white pairs and put up pin 47, cloth stitch the lefthand pair back through the gold passive and again twist the gold pair once and the white pair twice. Remove T10 and tension all the threads carefully. (This is the only time that you will work an edge pin in a torchon ground stitch, in furture you will work a proper footside.)

Return to the pair hanging from pin 46 and work the diagonal row of torchon ground putting up pins 48-52 inclusive. Now go back to where you left the white pair after working them through the gold inner passives at pin 47. Make a torchon ground stitch with the pair from pin 48 and put up pin 53, carry on working that line right down to pin 57. The pair from pin 53 now cloth stitches through the gold pair and is twisted twice before cloth stitching through the pair which had been left at pin 47. Twist both pairs twice and put up pin 58 to the left of both pairs, the lefthand of the two now works back through the gold passive (which is twisted once as usual) and is twisted twice before making the torchon ground stitch at the start of the next diagonal row (pins 59-62). The righthand pair from pin 59 will go back through the gold passive and make up the footside. The pair coming back through the gold passive after pin 63 will start the new row of ground for pins 64-66. Complete the rest of the ground in the same way. You are now ready to work the next fan so can repeat these instructions starting again at pin 1 omitting those instructions dealing with hanging in new pairs.

Left: Working diagram for Candle Flounce

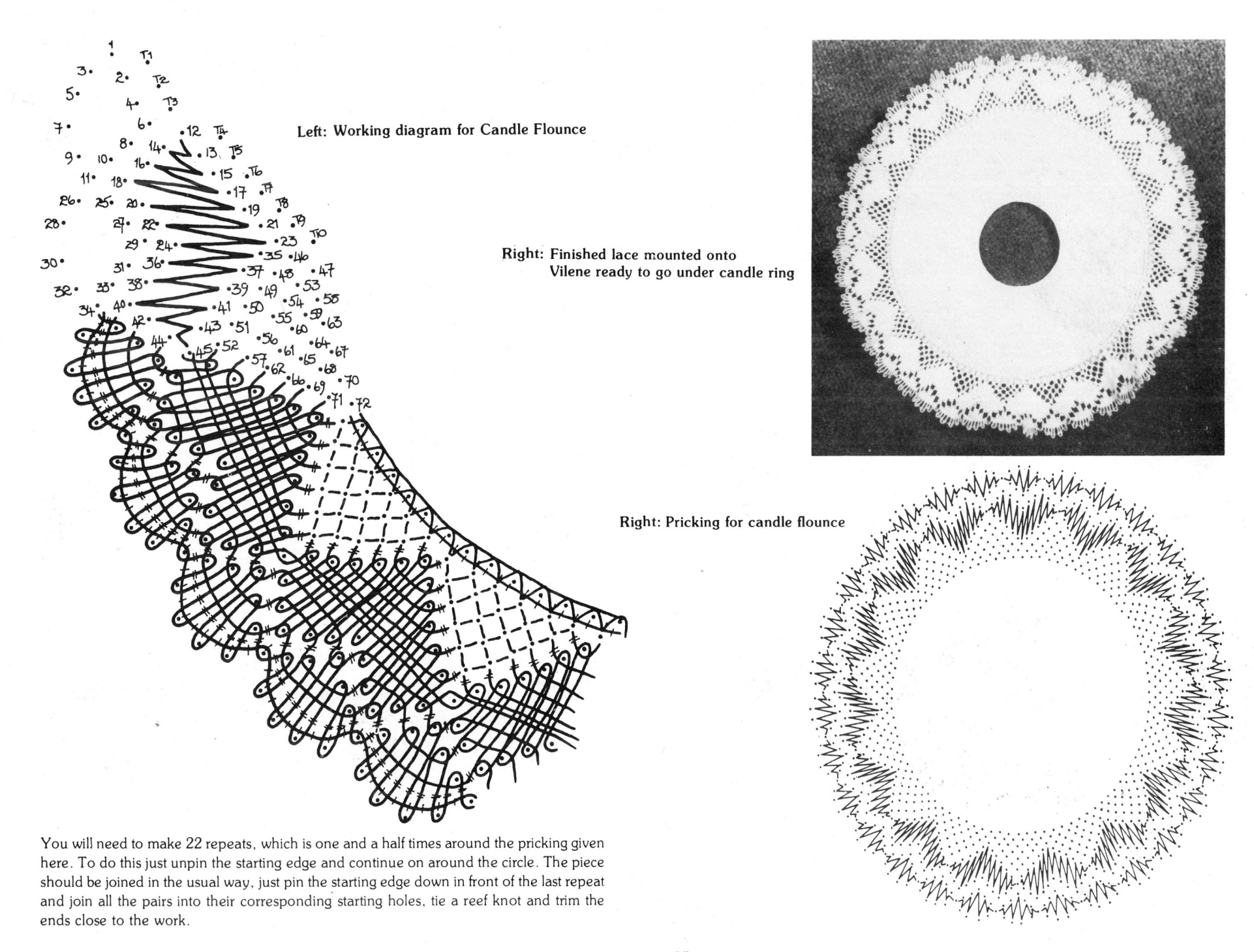

Right: Finished lace mounted onto Vilene ready to go under candle ring

Right: Pricking for candle flounce

You will need to make 22 repeats, which is one and a half times around the pricking given here. To do this just unpin the starting edge and continue on around the circle. The piece should be joined in the usual way, just pin the starting edge down in front of the last repeat and join all the pairs into their corresponding starting holes, tie a reef knot and trim the ends close to the work.

WEDDING PROJECTS

HEARTS, FLOWERS & FRAME PROJECTS

CHRISTMAS PROJECTS 37 CHRISTMAS PROJECTS

Above: Finished project

To mount it you will need a small piece of heavy-weight Vilene (non-woven interfacing used for stiffening in dress-making) alternatively you could bond two thicknesses of lighter weight Iron-On Vilene together to make a stiffer backing. Cut out a circle 3⅜" (8cm) in diameter. Cut a 1" (2.5cm) hole in the centre of this. Mark the half way and then quarter points on the outer edge of the backing circle, and using pins mark the quarter points on the inner edge of your lace. Match all four points, bringing the lace over the edge of the Vilene until it can be stitched in place without gathering (approximately 3/16" or 2mm). Using a length of white lace thread back stitch through the pinholes of the footside edge easing the lace wherever necessary so that the inner edge lies quite flat.

The candle flounce is now ready to take its place underneath your candle ring decoration.

FRAME EDGINGS

Here are two small circular edgings which I have used to frame small cross-stitch pictures. I have mounted one into a gilt frame and the other I used to decorate a calendar set in a commercial rectangular mount. I'm sure these designs could readily be used for greetings cards using a small picture as the centre-piece.

FINE TORCHON EDGING

In fact this is the same pricking which was used for the candle flounce, but for this piece it has been considerably reduced in size. To maintain the red worker for the heart shape you will notice that the worker goes alternately to the right and then to the left at the start of each heart. I chose not to work a proper footside on this piece, working torchon ground right up to the edge, but you are welcome to add the extra pair needed to work a footside if you prefer.

1 pair of red DMC 50 Brilliant as workers for the heart. Cut 1 3yd (3m) length.
1 pair of white 100/3 Brok (or 50 DMC) as workers for the fan. Cut 1 2yd (2m) length.
12 pairs of white 100/3 Brok (or equivalent) as passives. Cut 13 1yd (1m) lengths.
1 pair of red DMC 50 Brilliant as outside passives for the fan. Cut 1 1yd (1m) length.

WORKING INSTRUCTIONS

Hang the red passives on pin 1, followed by the white fan workers. Put the workers down to the right of the red pair and twist the two centre threads (one white and one red) twice lifting the bobbins right over left as usual. Now twist the red outside passives once and the workers twice. Hang three pairs of passives from pins T1, T2 and T3. You can now work the cloth stitch fan maintaining the usual pattern of twists — one on the outer passive, two on the workers between the red and white passives and two on the worker at the end of every row. Remove T1 once the new pair has been worked through twice and let it slide down to rest on the workers (don't tension it too hard or you will pull the workers downwards) remove T1 & T2 in the same way. Leave the workers at pin 11 and twist each of the passives coming out of the fan at pins 6, 8 and 10 twice.

To start the heart hang one pair of white passives on pin 12 and push it to the left. Hang the red workers from the same pin to the right of the previous pair, twist the centre two threads twice. Hang one pair of passives on each of pins T4-T9 inclusive. You can now work the first half of the heart shape following the markings indicated on the pricking. Twist the workers twice before putting up the pin at the end of every row and tension the passives very carefully each time. After working pin 24 you must work the second fan remembering to twist the passives twice as they come out of the fan before they enter the heart. Complete the heart-shape and twist the passives twice as they leave it so that they are ready to work the torchon ground (half stitch, pin, half stitch and twist).

Hang a pair of passives on T10 and work a ground stitch at pin 46 with the pair which left the heart after pin 23. Remove T10 and let the new thread slip down to rest snugly round the lower pin. Put T10 back into the same hole and hang on the final pair of passives, make a ground stitch at pin 47 before removing T10 and tensioning carefully. You can

Working Diagram for Fine Torchon Edging

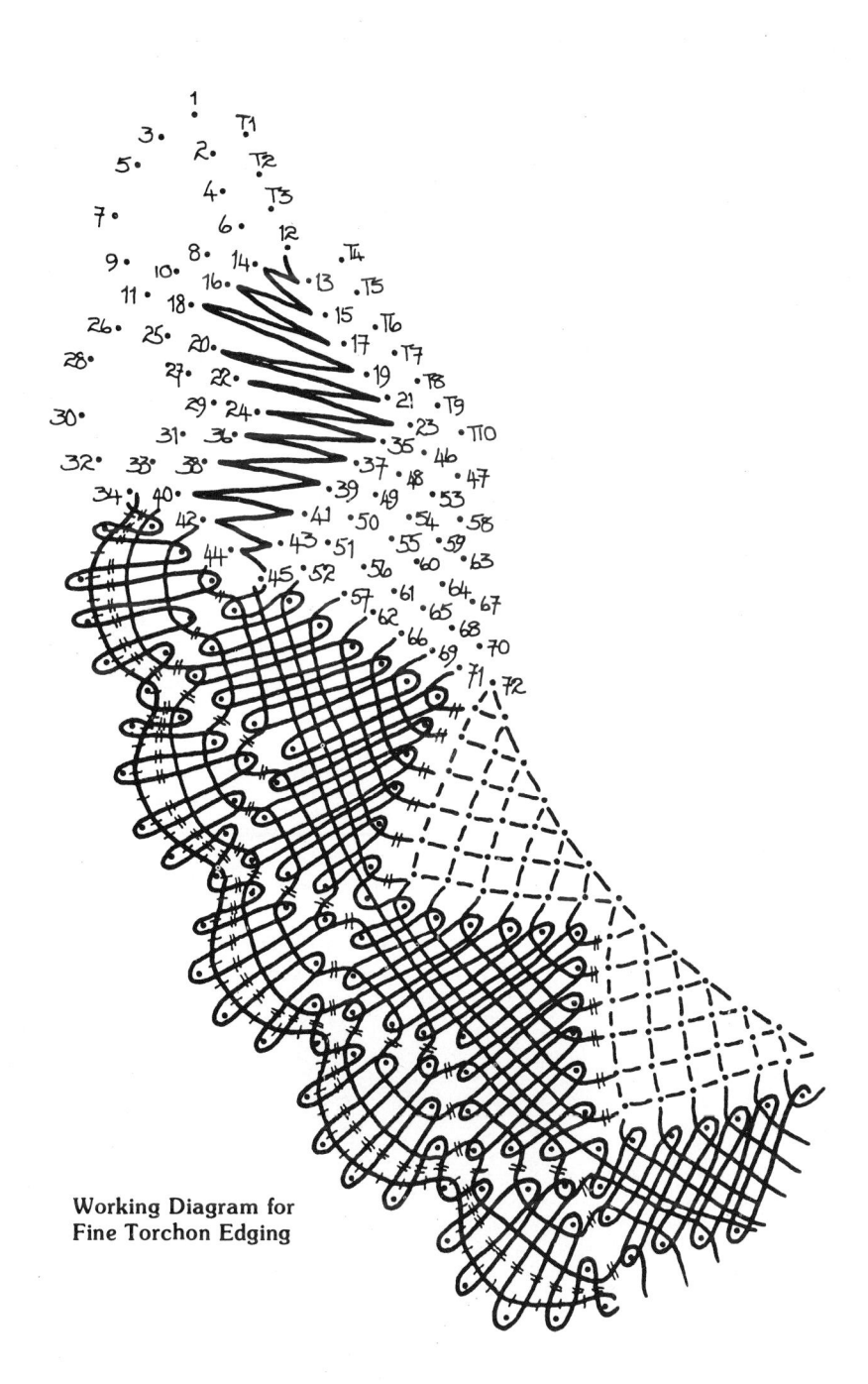

Above: Fine Torchon Edging mounted in a frame around a small cross stitch embroidery

now return to pin 46 and work the row of ground going diagonally between pins 48 and 52. Keep returning to the highest empty pinhole in the triangle of ground and working diagonal rows 53-57, 58-62, 63-66 etc, until the ground is complete. You are now ready to return to the outer edge to work the next fan.

Once the circle is complete you must join each pair into its corresponding starting loop, tie a reef knot and trim the ends close to the work. Choose the colour for your background card and cut out a circle which is precisely the same size as the centre circle of your lace. A touch of glue behind several of the red hearts will keep your lace in place against the card. Position the picture or embroidery in the centre of the cutout and glue it in place — it is easiest if you put a thin line of glue around the circle edge on the under surface of the background card, then put it down on top of the centre-piece, making sure that the design will be in the centre before pressing the card down firmly. Slip the card into your frame and reassemble it.

CHRISTMAS PROJECTS

Above: Pricking for Fine Torchon Edging

Below: Finished lace

40

A SIMPLE FLOWER CHRISTMAS CARD

Using the instructions in the Christmas Flower section (Page 49) make one large cloth stitch flower in Twilley's Gold Dust. Add five green leaf-shaped sequins and a red flower-shaped sequin and glue them into the circular inset of a commercial Christmas card. What could be simpler?

SIMPLE LEAF EDGING

This is a simple edging which for the first time introduces leaves. It looks very effective as a border against a darker background. It is obviously a more challenging piece so I shall assume that the lacemaker is conversant with such techniques as making a footside, windmills, leaves, 'broken' trail etc.

10 pairs of 100/3 Brok or similar fine cotton eg. DMC 50 Retors d'Alsace. Cut 10 4yd (4m) lengths.

Hang 2 pairs around pin 1 and interlink them. Twist both pairs twice, the lefthand pair will start off as the worker, the right remains as the footside pair. Hang one trail passive on each of pins T1 and T2, hang two pairs 'open' or 'astride' from a temporary pin (T3) positioned anywhere to the left of the footside trail. Take the worker and cloth stitch through the two trail passives and then the first pair only of the two hanging to the left. Twist the workers twice (as you will do at the end of every row) and put up pin 2. Work back through all three pairs and make up the footside in the usual way at pin 3. Remove pins T1 and T2 and tension the passives carefully so that they don't pull down on the workers. Remove T3 and use the two pairs hanging from it to make the first leaf towards pin 4. Put up pin 4 between the two pairs of the leaf and tension the leaf carefully.

Hang two new pairs astride T4 (positioned anywhere to the left of pin 4) and windmill the two new pairs with the two leaf pairs repositioning pin 4 at the centre. Remove T4 and tension the new pairs so that they rest neatly around pin 4. These will be your new leaf pairs, the pairs from the previous leaf becoming the passives in the outer trail.

Hang two pairs around pin 5, interlink them and twist both pairs once. The pair on the right will be the worker and will cloth stitch through the two pairs from the first leaf before twisting twice at the end of the row. Put up pin 6. Cloth stitch back through the two pairs, twist the worker once and cloth stitch through the outside passive which is always twisted once, twist the worker twice as usual because it is the end of the row and put up pin 7.

Leave the worker at pin 7 and go back to work the second leaf, park it astride pin 16. Now go back and complete the footside trail pins 8-15 inclusive. Bring the worker across through the footside passives and then cloth stitch them through both of the leaf pairs waiting at pin 16. Do not twist the worker. Take out pin 16 and put it up again between the two leaf pairs (ie. two pairs in from the left). Cover the pin using the two adjacent pairs (the two leaf pairs) and continue working to the right through the two footside passives (the lefthand leaf pair has become your new workers). Make up the footside as usual at pin 17. The two lefthand-most pairs will now be the new leaf pairs (one was the previous footside worker and the other was from the previous leaf). This technique will give you a nice sharp change of direction where the leaves meet the inner trail.

Now work the third leaf parking it astride pin 28, before returning to pin 7 and completing the outside trail (pins 18-27). Leave your workers at pin 27. Cloth stitch the lefthand leaf pair from pin 28 through the first two pairs of passives in the outer trail. Cloth stitch the righthand leaf pair through the innermost trail passive, take out pin 24 and reposition it with the two pairs from the last cloth stitch on its right. Cover the pin making a cloth stitch with the two adjacent pairs (the righthand pair from the leaf and the lefthand pair of the

Above Right: Finished Calendar

Below Right: Working Diagram for Simple Leaf Edging

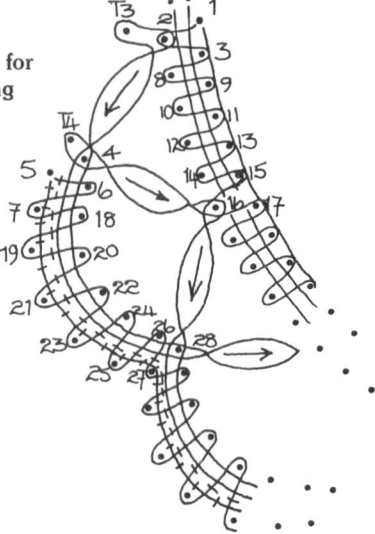

Above: Detail of Simple Leaf Edging & a small piece of cross stitch embroidery

Above: Pricking for Simple Leaf Edging

Below: Finished lace edging

two passives from the outer trail). The two pairs of passives from the outer trail will now work the next leaf and the leaf pairs will become the passives in the outer trail. A fine exchange!

Continue in this way until the circle is complete. Because this piece is to be used as a border glued to a backing I used the simplest of joins. Continue the outer trail using pins 5 and 6 again before tying a reef knot with each of the four pairs and trimming the ends really close to the work. The final leaf is joined to the footside trail in the usual way using pins 1, 2 and 3 again. Each pair is then tied in a reef knot putting an extra twist on the first half of the knot so that you can make a really tight knot without any slipping. Trim the ends close to the knot. The neater starting end of both the inner and outer trails can be glued in place over the knots of the finishing edges once the pins are taken out and the lace removed from the pillow.

To make the calendar illustrated here I cut a piece of card large enough to fill the cutout of a commercial card mount. The mount itself was 7" x 9" (18cm x 23cm) with a cutout of 4⅜" x 6⅜" (11cm x 16cm), the background card 5" x 7¼" (12.5cm x 18.5cm). I cut a small circle out of the background card 1½" (4cm) from the top edge, 1⅞" (4.7cm) in diameter. Using small touches of glue behind the footside trail glue the lace around the edge of the circle cutout. Glue the under side of the circle cutout close to the edge and lower it onto your picture, photograph, or in this case a small piece of fine cross stitch embroidery. Glue the background card to the mount and complete the project by adding a small calendar. If you wish to hang it up then add a loop of ribbon at the top, alternatively you could cover the back of the mount with a matching piece of card, adding a further double thickness of card as a 'prop' to make a free-standing calendar.

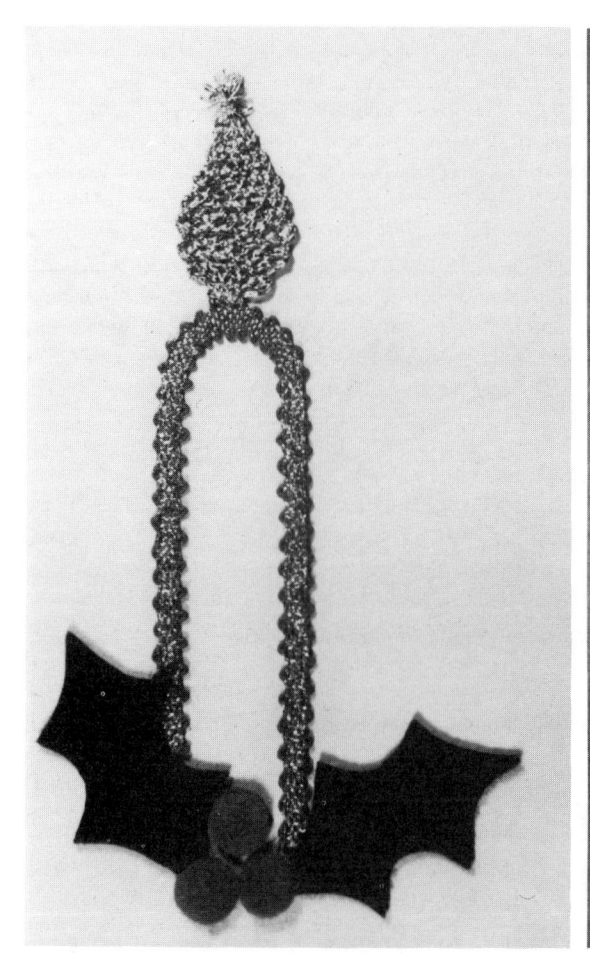

A TAPE LACE CANDLE.

1 pair of DMC Coton Perlé No. 8. Cut 1 70" (175cm) length.
3 pairs of Twilley's Gold Dust.
  Cut 3 30" (75cm) lengths if you do not intend to work a flame in lace.
  Cut 3 45" (115cm) lengths if you intend to work a flame in the same thread.

This very simple candle shape makes an ideal beginner's piece as it requires very few bobbins and is worked entirely in cloth stitch. Even very young inexperienced children can make a good job of this. Colour is an important part of this project and children can be encouraged to choose their own colour scheme although a combination of red Perlé workers with gold passives is hard to beat!

When finished the candle makes an attractive Christmas card or it can be used as a calendar inscribed 'To light you through the year'.

Far Left: Card with felt leaves & berries
Left: Calendar with commercial leaves, sequin berries & tinsel flame

WORKING INSTRUCTIONS

Position the pricking in the very centre of the pillow, pin it in place with a pin at each corner and press those pins right down into the pillow. Place your cover cloth across the pillow so that about 1½" (3-4cm) of the start is showing, pin it in place positioning the pins out to the side well away from the working area.

Wind the pairs taking care to put half of the thread onto each bobbin of the pair. Hang one pair of the Gold Dust passives onto each of pins 1, 2 & 3; and the Perlé workers onto pin 4. Cloth stitch across through the 3 pairs of passives, twist the workers twice and put up pin 5. Now tension the work very carefully. First pull the workers tight and keep them tight with one hand whilst the other pulls gently on each of the passives until the whole row lies smooth and flat. Continue working to and fro remembering to put two twists on the workers at the end of every row and checking that these twists are made correctly. The only other potential error is the possibility of getting the passives out of order. If this is a child's first piece then you might like to 'rig' the bobbins selected for the passive pairs. To do this choose bobbins of distinctly different colours or designs and wind each pair with matching bobbins, so that if threads of adjacent pairs become twisted the lacemaker will notice that the bobbins are no longer in the correct order and that she must look for an error. Try to encourage the lacemaker to look very closely at the work whilst tensioning the passives at the end of every row, watch out for twists and crosses which should not be there!

Take care around the top curve of the candle as the inner holes become much closer together and it's easy to miss one, so keep checking that the workers are in step with the zigzag marking on the pricking.

As the second side of the candle is worked the pins of the first side will get in the way, so press down every third pin on each side of the work and remove the remaining pins. Keep re-positioning the cover cloth ahead of the work so that the bobbins are always lying on a smooth surface and the heads of the pins which have been pushed down into the pillow cannot catch the threads as work continues.

To finish the piece take the workers to the last pinhole and slip one worker thread behind that last pin and one below it. Using a reef knot with an extra twist on the first part, tie the workers around the pin. Tie a reef knot with each passive pair, cut off the ends close to the work. If you are planning to work the flame of your candle in lace leave your outline securely pinned to the pillow and follow the instructions for working the flame. If not, then you can remove the pins, keeping the lace pressed down onto the pillow with one hand whilst you take the pins out one at a time with the other. Use a pinlifter to raise the pins which were pressed down into the pillow.

Your candle outline may tend to twist once all the pins are removed, but don't try to press it or pull it. Decide how you wish to mount it and glue it carefully to your background. It is best to use a glue such as Bostik, but it should always be used extremely sparingly. Start by gluing the curved portion of the candle and pressing that down into position before gluing an inch or so of the straight part at a time and pressing that down as you go. Make sure that the second side of the candle is parallel to the first.

Templates for holly leaves which can be cut from felt or green tinsel

Templates for tinsel flames. Cut the larger shape in gold & the smaller in red.

Above: Pricking for Tape Lace candle & Half Stitch flame

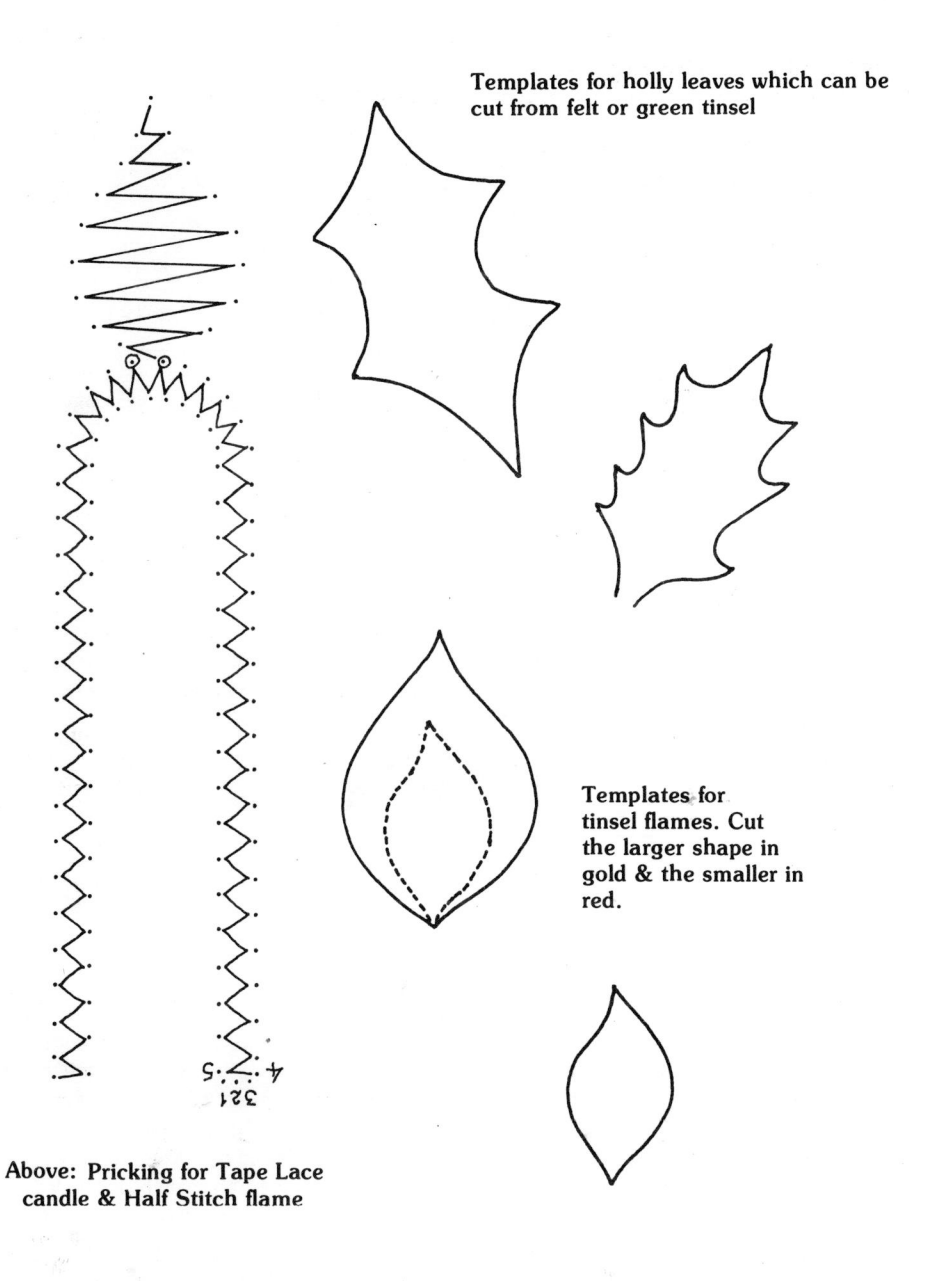

There are two ways of making the candle flame, you can either use gold and red paper-backed foil to cut out two flame shapes which are glued into place using 'Copydex, a paper gum or a craft glue which does not destroy the surface of the tinsel, or you can work your flame in half stitch which is obviously a little more difficult.

If you have used gold passives for your candle you can use the leftover lengths to work your flame. Take the two pins out of the holes at the top of the candle which were marked with a circle so that you can 'sew' the new threads into the loop of the worker threads formed around the circled pins. Take one of the leftover lengths of thread and fold it in half. Use a crochet hook to pull the loop of the new thread through the worker loops at one of the circled pinholes. Pass the ends through that loop and pull it tight. Do the same at the second pinhole. Now wind on the bobbins and replace the two pins. Divide the remaining 4 pieces of thread into two and wind half onto each bobbin.

Push the pair hanging from the lefthand circled pin to the left, then put in a new pin between the two circled ones and hang one pair of bobbins on it, push those bobbins to the left and hang a second pair around the same pin, push those to the left and hang on a third and then a fourth pair in the same way. You are now ready to start working the flame.

Take the lefthand-most pair as your workers and half stitch through the 5 pairs of passives to the right, at the end of the row twist the two righthand threads twice more which will make a total of 3 twists on those threads, then put up a pin. Half stitch back across the row in the same way. You will find that you have a different thread going all the way across the row each time, so that all your threads will be used evenly. However should any bobbin run short of thread you can avoid using it as a 'worker' by adjusting the number of twists at the end of the row. To do this make sure that the bobbin with the most thread on (of the 2 outermost bobbins) ends up closest to the work (rather than being in the outside position) after the twists are in place. If it is not, then simply remove one of the twists. The outermost bobbin with the least thread on it is then left behind as a passive.

At the tip of the flame put up the last pin as usual, now take the bobbin which has come all the way across from the other side and the bobbin which is on the extreme righthand side and tie the first half of a reef knot putting on an extra twist. You may find it easier to remove the two bobbins from the threads in order to tie this knot. Now lift all the passive threads in a bunch in one hand and bring the righthand knot thread underneath all the passives to the lefthand side and vice versa. Put the passives down and bring the 2 knot threads to the top and tie a complete reef knot pulling the passives into a nice tight bunch. Tension all of the passive threads one last time and trim off about ¼" (5mm) away from the knot. Trim the knot threads to a similar length. All the pins can now be removed.

To complete the project you need to add some holly leaves and a bunch of berries. You can buy commercially produced holly leaves in gold, silver or green, but if you prefer you can cut out a leaf shape from green felt. The berries can also be cut from felt, or you can use some red sequins, the 'cup-shaped' 8mm sequins look nicer than the flat shape. You can experiment with various arrangements of the leaves and berries as long as you position them in such a way that they cover the ends of your candle outline.

The candle was mounted on a piece of card 3¼" x 8¼" (8cm x 20.5cm) to make a calendar, a 3½" (8.5cm) length of red satin ribbon was used to make a hanging loop and two 1" (2.5cm) lengths attached the calendar to the lower edge.

For the Christmas card use a piece of card approximately 8" x 6¼" (20cm x 15.5cm) which is folded in half to give a finished card 4" wide and 6¼" tall (10cm x 15.5cm). Before you decide on the final dimensions make sure you have an envelope into which it will fit!

Left: Working Diagram for Circular Torchon Edging

Above: Pricking for Circular Torchon Edging

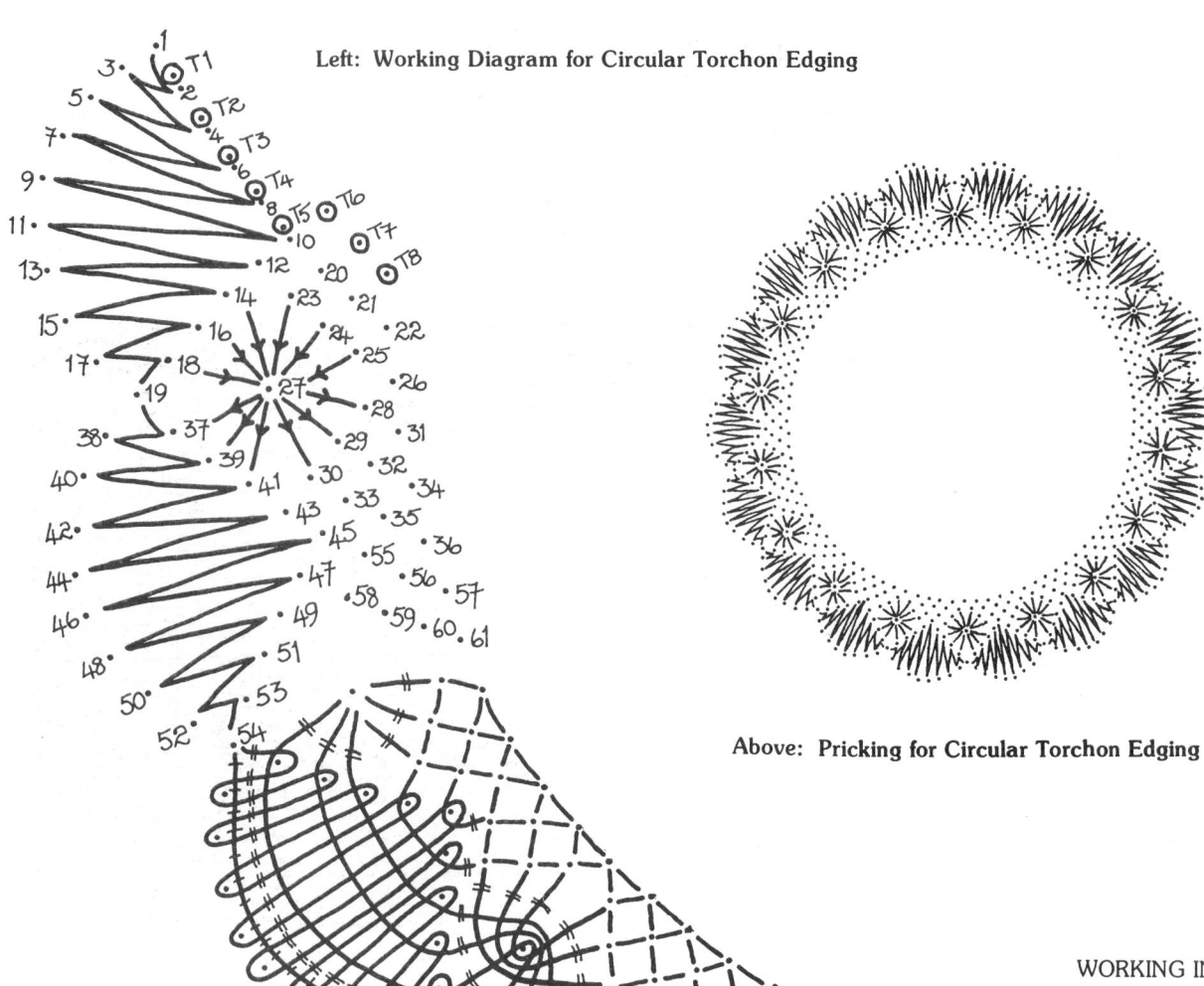

Above: Finished lace decorating a Christmas card

CIRCULAR TORCHON EDGING.

8 pairs of Mez Effektgarn or equivalent in gold or silver. Cut 8 40" (100cm) lengths.
1 pair of red DMC 30 Brilliant. Cut 1 130" (325cm) length.
1 pair of green DMC 30 Brilliant. Cut 1 130" (325cm) length.

This is a fine torchon edging where the pinholes are quite close together, a good working knowledge of fans, spiders and torchon ground is therefore advisable. If more experience of such features is needed it is better to choose a larger scale pattern such as the skirt trimming for the larger angel.

WORKING INSTRUCTIONS

Hang one pair of gold passives onto each of the temporary pins T1-8. Hang the red worker on pin 1 and push them towards the right, hang the green workers from the same pin but place them to the left of the red ones, make a cloth stitch with both pairs, now twist the red pair once (this will be the outside passive for this fan) and the green pair twice (this will be the worker). Cloth stitch the worker through the gold pair from T1 and twist the worker twice because it is the end of the row, put up pin 2. Cloth stitch back towards pin 3 remembering to twist the worker twice before cloth stitching through the outside passive. Twist the passive once and the worker twice as usual, put up pin 3. Continue the fan taking in one new passive from each of the temporary pins before working pins 4, 6, 8 & 10. Complete the fan leaving out one gold passive pair after working pins 10, 12, 14, 16 & 18. Work pin 19 with a torchon ground stitch (half stitch, pin, half stitch and twist). This enables the outside passive and the worker to exchange places and the next fan will be worked with a green outside passive and a red worker.

All the gold pairs leaving the fan from pins 10, 12, 14, 16, & 18 must now be twisted twice. The pairs from 14, 16 & 18 will form the spider's legs and the pairs from 10 & 12 will go into the ground. To work the torchon ground take the gold pair from T5 which has left the fan after pin 10 and work a half stitch with the pair hanging from T6, put up pin 20, complete the ground stitch with another half-stitch and twist. The righthand pair from pin 20 now goes through the same process with the pair from T7. Repeat for pin 22 using the pair from T8. When pins 20, 21 & 22 are in place remove pins T6, T7 & T8 and ease the pairs down to rest snugly around pins 20-22. Continue working pins 23-26 using the same half stitch, pin, half stitch and twist.

Now work the spider using the pairs from pins 14, 16, 18, 23, 24 & 25. Check that each leg has been twisted twice before you begin (the pairs from pins 23, 24 & 25 should already have 2 twists from the torchon ground and the pairs from 14, 16 & 18 were twisted twice after they left the fan). To make the spider take the pair from pin 14 and cloth stitch it through the three legs to its right (from pins 23, 24 & 25) cloth stitch the pair from pin 16 through the same three legs, and do the same with the pair from pin 18. Put up pin 27 in the middle of the spider. Take the pair from the immediate left of the pin and cloth stitch it through the three pairs to its right. Now take the next pair from the lefthand group and cloth stitch it through the same three pairs from the right. Repeat with the final pair from the left of the pin. All six pairs should now be back on the same side as they started from. Twist each pair twice to complete the spider.

'Fence' the spider in by working pins 28, 29 & 30 in the usual torchon ground stitch. Work pins 31-36 in the same ground stitch. Now return to the edge and work the next fan (pins 37-54). Complete the torchon ground area (pins 55-61) and you are then ready to begin work on the next spider. Repeat pins 27-61 until the circle is complete.

To join the circle sew the ground pairs into the corresponding temporary pinholes along the edge of the fan (pins T1-T5) and the remaining 3 pairs into pinholes 20, 21 & 22. Both the green and red workers will sew into pin 1. Reef knot each pair neatly, remove the bobbins, take out all the pins and then trim the ends as close to the work as possible.

MOUNTING

Select a suitable card mount, or make a card of your own using a piece of card 10½" x 4½" (26.25cm x 11.25cm). Fold the card into 3 equal sections to make a finished card 3½" wide and 4½" tall (8.75cm x 11.25cm). In the centre section mark a circle 2¼" (5.5cm) in diameter 1" (2.5cm) away from the top edge. Cut this circle out piercing the card well inside the circle and slowly cutting in a spiral fashion until you smoothly meet the drawn line of the circle. Glue the lace onto the card putting small touches of glue behind each fan. Now select a suitable picture to fit inside the circle, it could be from an old Christmas or birthday card, or a photograph. Alternatively you could slip a rectangle of contrasting coloured card or fabric down behind the cut out circle and use it as a background for a second piece of lace.

SMALL TORCHON CANDLE.

14 pairs of DMC 100 Cordonnet Special or equivalent. Cut 14 18" (45cm) lengths.
1 pair of Twilley's Gold Dust as a gimp. Cut 1 24" (60cm) length.

This is a piece of fine torchon, which because of its fine scale makes a most attractive Christmas card. To work it successfully you must be familiar with torchon ground, spiders and working with a gimp. It is possible to enlarge this pattern and work it with a thicker thread.

Above: Christmas card with small torchon candle

Above: Pricking for small torchon candle

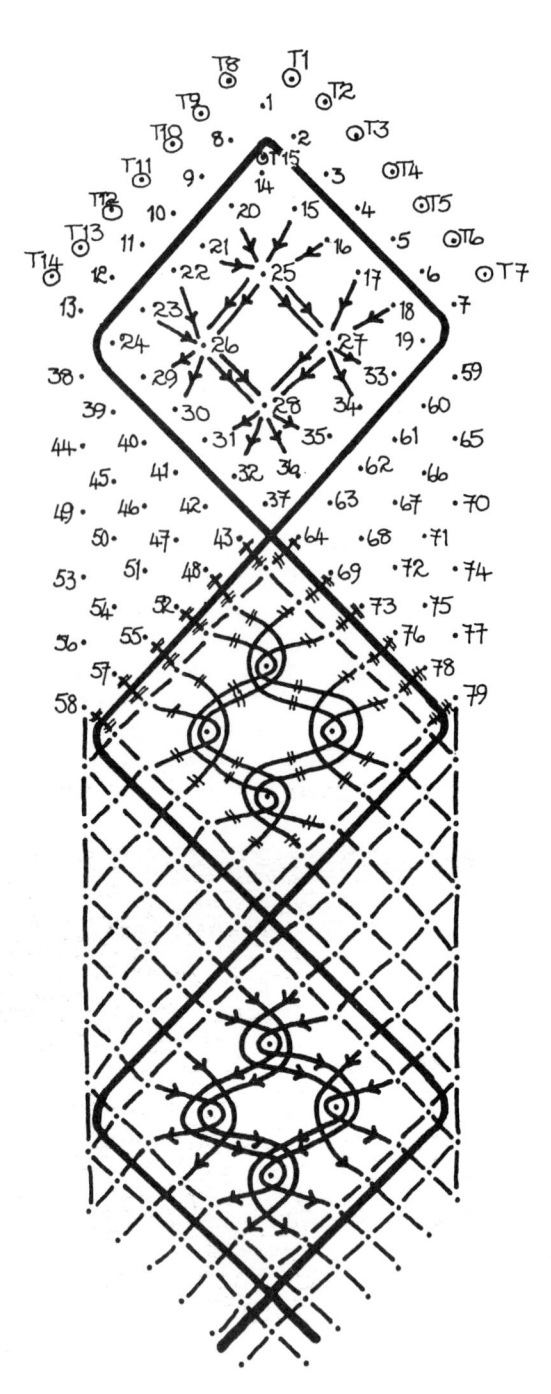

Working Diagram for small torchon candle

WORKING INSTRUCTIONS

Wind half of each length of thread onto a bobbin. Hang one pair of white bobbins on each of pins T1-T14. Using the pairs from T1 and T8 work a torchon ground stitch (half stitch, pin, half stitch and twist) putting up pin 1. Remove pins T1 & T8 and tension the pairs at pin 1. Continue working torchon ground stitches at pins 2-7 using one pair from each temporary pin in turn (T2-T7) and the pair originally from T8 (and now the righthand pair from pin 1) which will work diagonally along the whole top edge on this side of the candle. Return to the pair left at pin 1 (originally from T1) and work a torchon ground stitch with that and the pair from T9, putting up pin 8. Continue working down that lefthand edge putting up pins 8-13. Now remove all of the remaining temporary pins (T2-7 & T9-14) and tension all the pairs carefully.

Put up temporary pin T15 and hang the gold gimp around it. Work the righthand gimp bobbin through all the pairs hanging from pins 2-6 inclusive and the lefthand of the two pairs hanging from pin 7. Work the lefthand gimp bobbin through all the pairs hanging from pins 8-12 inclusive and the righthand pair hanging from pin 13. There will be no need to put extra twists on the pairs coming from the torchon ground stitches before the gimp but you must remember to twist each white pair twice after the gimp has passed through. (To work the gimp through a pair simply lift the lefthand bobbin and pass the gimp bobbin through. It is always the lefthand bobbin which is lifted regardless of which direction the gimp is coming from.) Work pins 14-24 inclusive all in torchon ground. Now work the block of 4 two-legged spiders and complete the diamond with torchon ground pins 29-37. Now work the gimp threads inwards and downwards towards the point of the diamond and cross the righthand gimp thread over the top of the left. Complete the larger areas of torchon ground pins 38-79 inclusive. Making sure that the gimps are correctly crossed, pass them through the pairs from the pins bordering the lower edge of the torchon ground areas.

Now repeat from pin 14-79 until all 4 diamonds are complete. Work a little extra torchon ground at the end and then tie off all the pairs with a reef knot at each pin. The gimps can be cut off without knotting. Remove the pins.

MOUNTING

I used a dark green coloured card with a rectangular cut out standing on its longer edge. Arrange the candle to one side of the card tucking the finished edge under the border. Before gluing the lace in place check that there is sufficient room for the candle flame and for the paper 'Merry Christmas'. Now add a pair of small sized holly leaves in gold or silver to match your gimp, an embroidered motif to give the effect of 3 holly berries and a small red and gold paper tinsel flame to complete the project. If you prefer you can use a gold or silver effect felt pen to add your greeting.

**Templates for small torchon candle flame
Cut the larger in gold & the smaller in red**

CHRISTMAS FLOWERS.

You can make a wide variety of flowers using glittery threads in both cloth stitch and half stitch. I used two sizes of flowers to decorate an assortment of gift tags, bags and boxes.

1. Small Flowers in Cloth Stitch.

If you are working in a combination of Twilley's Gold Dust and DMC Perlé No 8 cut the following lengths:-

4 pairs of passives in either type of thread. Cut 4 16" (40cm) lengths.
1 pair of workers preferably in DMC Perlé. Cut 1 50" (125cm) length.

If you are working entirely in Twilley's Gold Dust cut the following lengths:

3 pairs of glittery passives. Cut 3 16" (40cm) lengths.
1 pair of glittery workers. Cut 1 50" (125cm) length.

These flowers are easily and quickly worked so are an ideal project for younger children.

WORKING INSTRUCTIONS

Hang the workers on the inside edge pin and the three or four pairs of passives from the two temporary pins marked on the pattern. Make sure that the threads are hung in the correct order if you intend to have an outside passive of a contrasting colour. Make sure that the two bobbins of each pair are lying side by side.

Take the worker pair and cloth stitch across through the inner passives (three if you are using Perlé and Gold Dust, two if you are using only Gold Dust). Twist the workers once before cloth stitching through the outside passive pair and twice afterwards because it is the end of the row. Put up the edge pin and tension all the threads carefully. Work back across the row remembering to twist the workers once between the outer and the inner group of passives. When the workers reach the inner edge again two twists are sufficient if you are using Perlé workers, twist Gold Dust workers three times before putting up the pin. (Remember to remove the temporary pins after the first two rows and tension the passives so that they rest snugly against the worker.) Continue in this way until you have completed all five petals.

FINISHING

The workers finish at the inner edge pin, but do not twist them before putting up the pin, simply slip one worker thread above the edge pin and one below it and tie a reef knot around the pin putting an extra twist onto the first half of the knot which will prevent it slipping before you tie the second half in the usual way. Now tie off each pair of passives with a reef knot and trim the passives close to the knot. DO NOT trim off the workers unless they are Gold Dust which is not really strong enough to use as a gathering thread. Remove the worker bobbins and take out all the pins. Using the longer of the Perlé worker threads or a doubled length of toning sewing cotton sew alternately up and down through the edge loops of the straight edge. Now pull up the gathering thread as tightly as you can and make a double backstitch at the end so that it cannot slacken. Lap the neater starting edge over the knots of the finishing edge and stab stitch up and down through the two thicknesses until they are securely joined. Finish off with an extra backstitch on the back of the flower and trim off any remaining threads. Now ease the gathers evenly around the flower and it's ready for use!

2. Small Flowers in Half Stitch.

4 pairs of Twilley's Gold Dust. Cut 4 26" (65cm) lengths.

WORKING INSTRUCTIONS

Using the same pricking used for the small cloth stitch flower hang one pair on the inner edge pin as the worker, two on one temporary pin and one on the other. Work entirely in half stitch simply adding two extra twists to the workers at the end of every row. Finish and join in exactly the same way as the cloth stitch flower.

3. Large Flowers in Cloth Stitch.

5 pairs of Twilley's Gold Dust passives. Cut 5 20" (50cm) lengths.
1 pair of Twilley's Gold Dust workers. Cut 1 80" (200cm) length.

WORKING INSTRUCTIONS

Hang the workers on the inner edge pin and the 5 pairs of passives from temporary pins above the first row. Cloth stitch through the three pairs of inner passives and then twist the workers once between each of the next two pairs of passives. Twist the workers twice at the scalloped end of the row and three times at the straight edge before putting up the pin. Don't forget to remove the temporary pins after the first two rows and tension all the passives carefully.

Prickings for small & large flowers

Gift boxes decorated with one simple flower and miniature holly leaves

Christmas Gift Tag

Template for tinsel background

Pricking for smallest half-stitch circle

Finished card showing smallest half-stitch circle mounted on tinsel background with snowflake shaped sequin.

Working entirely in Gold Dust does require more care when tensioning, because the threads do not slide very smoothly against each other, so make sure that your work is flat and even before proceeding with the next row.

Follow the same finishing instructions given for the small cloth stitch flower.

4. Large Flowers in Half Stitch.

7 pairs of Twilley's Gold Dust. Cut 7 24" (60cm) lengths.

WORKING INSTRUCTIONS

Use the same pricking as for the large cloth stitch flower and hang one pair on the pin at the top of the straight inner edge. The remaining 6 pairs of passives are hung from temporary pins spread out above the working line. Now follow exactly the same instructions as given for the small half stitch flower.

MOUNTING

To make a gift tag cut a 4" x 2" (10cm x 5cm) piece of card and fold it in half. Glue one small flower into the corner, then arrange three small holly leaves as shown in the example. You can cut these holly leaves out yourself or you can buy a small triangular arrangement of three tiny holly leaves which can be cut apart and tucked under the edge of the flower. You can write a greeting using a gold or silver effect felt pen.

You can make a similar arrangement on the side, or on the lid of a small gift box, adding a commercial paper Christmas greeting.

The gift bag is decorated with two small and one large gold flower. A variety of silver leaf-shaped sequins complete the arrangement.

Don't forget that when gluing onto a foil covered box you must make sure that the glue is used sparingly and that no glue touches the surface of the foil where it will not be hidden by the decoration.

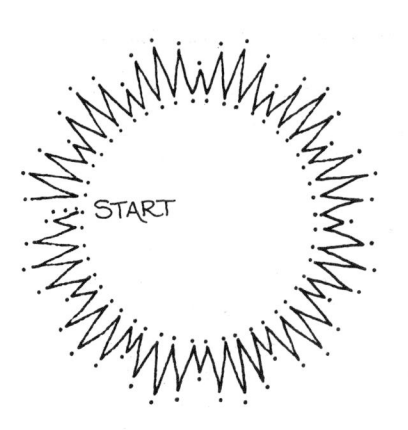

HALF STITCH CIRCLES.

1. Smallest Half Stitch Circle.

4 pairs of Twilley's Gold Dust. Cut 4 40" (110cm) lengths.

This is a very simple piece worked entirely in half stitch, making it a good project on which to learn or practise this stitch.

WORKING INSTRUCTIONS

Wind half of each length of thread onto each bobbin. Put one pin into the hole on the inner edge of the circle as marked on the pattern. Place three more pins quite close together along the working line drawn from the inner pinhole to the outer edge. Hang one pair from each pin. Take the righthand pair as your workers and half stitch across to the left through all the passives. At the end of the row add two more twists to the workers (making a total of three altogether as of course one twist is already there as part of the final half stitch). Put up the edge pin and work back in half stitch remembering to put two **extra** twists on the workers at the end of the row before putting up the inner edge pin. Tension well at the end of every row.

Putting 2 extra twists on the workers at the end of the row will constantly change the one thread which works all the way from one side to the other. This should ensure that each thread is used evenly, but should one thread run short you can avoid using it as the worker by putting on only one additional twist at the end of the row instead of the usual two. (When the workers are twisted and the edge pin is in place it is the thread which is nearest that pin which will go all the way across, so ensure that this is the bobbin with the most thread by adjusting the number of twists if necessary at the edge of the work.)

50

FINISHING

The final row will bring the workers to the inner edge pin (from which they originally started), bring one of the two worker threads through this starting loop and tie the two together around the pin with a reef knot. The other passives are finished off in the same way by bringing one thread of each pair through the corresponding starting loop and tying a reef knot. Remove the bobbins, take out the pins and trim the ends close to the knots.

MOUNTING

To make this into a small Christmas card or gift tag cut out a scalloped piece of paper-backed tinsel using the outline shown. Glue this to the centre of a 3" (7.5cm) square card (cut card 6" x 3" (15cm x 7.5cm) and fold it in half), glue the lace in place and add the finishing touch with a silver sequin in the shape of a snowflake. Don't forget that the foil must be glued in place with gum or Copydex. The lace and the sequin will have to be glued with a chemical glue such as Bostik, so take great care to use only the smallest amount at the widest points of the lace scallops and the very centre of the snowflake so that the effect of the glue on the foil will be completely hidden.

2. Medium Half Stitch Circle.

5 pairs of Twilley's Gold Dust. Cut 5 45" (115cm) lengths.
1 pair of Twilley's Gold Dust in a contrasting colour. Cut 1 28" (70cm) length.

3. Large Half Stitch Circle.

6 pairs of Twilley's Gold Dust. Cut 6 55" (140cm) lengths.
1 pair of Twilley's Gold Dust in a contrasting colour. Cut 1 48" (120cm) length.

These two pieces give plenty of opportunity to practise half stitch with a double half stitch (or cloth stitch and twist) ensuring that the contrasting coloured pair forms the outline of the scalloped edge. More experienced workers can cope with an extra pair of passives in each of these patterns should they prefer a denser effect.

WORKING INSTRUCTIONS

Hang the single contrasting coloured pair at the lefthand end of the row of setting up pins marked on the pattern. Hang one pair of bobbins on each of the other pins, the final pair will go on the innermost pinhole at the edge of the circle and this pair will start off as the workers.

Half stitch across the row from the inner edge towards the scallops of the outer edge until you come to the contrasting coloured pair, work a double half stitch ie. 2 half stitches, with this pair and the workers. (If you prefer you can think of this as a cloth stitch and twist which works out to be exactly the same.) Now put two extra twists on the worker pair (making a total of 3 twists altogther) and put up the edge pin. Work back across the row putting a similar double half stitch on the worker and contrasting coloured pair and half stitching through the rest of the passives. Twist the workers twice more at the end of the row and put up the pin as usual.

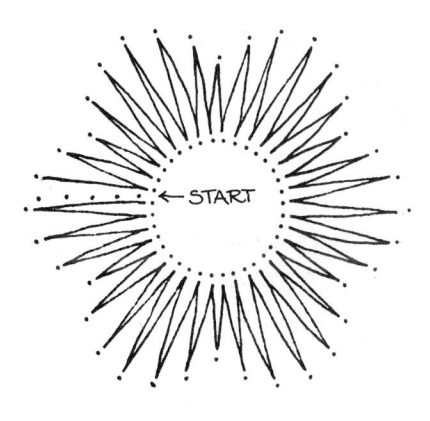

Above: Pricking for medium sized half-stitch circle

Right: Pricking for large sized half-stitch circle

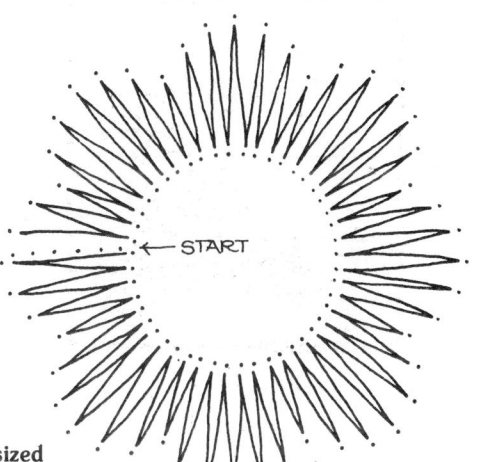

Below: Finished card showing medium circle with added flower & leaf-shaped sequins.

Finished calendar decorated with large half-stitch circle
& flower-shaped sequins

Take great care with your tensioning as the passives are closely spaced and the inner edge will be too crowded unless you pull up well at the end of every row.

At the end of every row check that the contrasting coloured pair is still in the correct position at the outer edge. If it is not, then you must go back and put it right taking care that the double half stitch is done correctly.

The holes at the inner edge of the piece are closely spaced and it is easy to miss some if you are careless, so make sure that you are always following the zigzag marking on the pattern exactly.

FINISHING

The worker will finish at the pinhole at the inner edge from which it started, so using a crochet hook or a lazy susan bring one of the worker threads through the starting loop at that pinhole and tie a reef knot around the pin. Each of the passive pairs is joined to the appropriate starting loop in exactly the same way. Remove the bobbins, take out the pins and trim the ends close to the knots.

An alternative method is to continue working, using the first three pinholes again so that the end of the work overlaps the starting edge. Having worked one extra pinhole at the outer edge and two extra pinholes at the inner edge, join the worker pair into the inner edge pinhole and tie a reef knot, all the rest of the passives can now simply be tied with a reef knot and cut off. This is obviously a much easier method but it is only acceptable because the piece will be glued down to a card background and all of the ends will be completely hidden behind the overlap.

MOUNTING

Choose the sequins you are going to use to decorate the circle. On the smaller circle I used all red sequins, and on a larger circle I used alternate red and green flower-shaped sequins. Thread a needle with a piece of fine thread matching the colour of the background half stitch and you are ready to stitch on the sequins. For added sparkle I stitched a tiny bead into the centre of each sequin. Bead and sequin can be stitched on together by bringing the needle up through the centre of the sequin, threading a tiny bead onto the needle (make sure that the needle is fine enough to go through the beads you are using) and then stitching back down the centre hole of the sequin. Run the needle through the back of the work until you reach the centre of the next scallop and repeat the process.

The lace is then glued to a background card of appropriate size and shape. The centre part of the calendar is a 3" (7.5cm) square mounted on a larger 4½" (11.25cm) square in a contrasting colour. 4" (10cm) of red ribbon was used to make a hanging loop and two 1" (2.5cm) lengths attached the calendar to the lower edge. The smaller lace circle was glued to the centre of a 3¾" (9.5cm) square of card and then 6 gold leaf-shaped sequins were glued at the V between each scallop.

DECORATED CHRISTMAS BALLS

You can buy quite a variety of silk-covered Christmas balls to hang on the Christmas tree, and it's nice to add a piece of lace to give a more unusual and eye-catching effect. The larger patterns I have designed to fit a ball with a 2¼" (5.5cm) diameter, but obviously those with a small pattern repeat can very readily be adapted to fit slightly larger or smaller ones. There's no need to use a tape measure to find the exact circumference of the ball you intend to use, simply wind a piece of ribbon around the widest part of the ball and add about ½" (1cm) for a small overlap, then run the ribbon down the side of the pattern and mark the length you need to make.

Simple Cloth Stitch Strip.

A narrow strip of the simplest whole stitch can look really effective when made in colourful and glittery threads. A piece just long enough to go round the smallest sized ball can be a very useful first project for beginners starting their first term of lace in September!

3 pairs of Twilley's Gold Dust passives. Cut 3 16" (40cm) lengths.
1 pair of DMC Coton Perlé No 8 workers. Cut 1 36" (100cm) length.

To help the beginner avoid accidental twists on the passives you can choose passives in two colours and alternate the pairs, or you can arrange for adjacent pairs of bobbins to be of a distinctly contrasting colour and decoration. Twist the workers twice at the end of every row and ensure that the passives are well-tensioned so that a nice, even strip of cloth stitch is produced.

When the required length has been worked tie a reef knot with the workers around the last edge pin, putting an extra twist on the first half of the reef knot prevents the threads from loosening before you complete the second half in the usual way. Tie a reef knot with each of the passive pairs and then trim off all the ends close to the knots. Take out the pins and you are ready to glue the lace to the ball.

Start by gluing the finishing end to the middle of the ball and continue gluing about an inch or so at a time. The neater starting edge will lap over the end and cover the final knots.

If the ball has a ring to which you can attach a loop use a 3" (7.5cm) length of leftover glitter thread. Some of the balls come with a very weak thread loop which children invariably manage to dislodge, to replace this in a more secure manner take a small piece of brass wire left over from spangling, and form it into a small crossed loop, slip the loop of thread onto the wire and slide it along until it reaches the centre, tighten the wire loop with pliers until it is small enough to slip through the hole in the top of the ball. Trim the ends of the wire to about ½" (1cm) and push one end into the hole and continue pushing and poking until the whole piece of wire is inside the ball. (Be sure to hold onto the loop of thread whilst you do this.) Now pull on the thread loop and the wire will position itself with the loop in the hole and give you a much sturdier hanger.

Pricking for simplest strip

Above: Finished Christmas balls decorated with simple cloth stitch strips

Below: Inserting a wire hanging loop into a Christmas ball

6 TRIMS FOR CHRISTMAS BALLS.

Before starting any of these patterns check the size of the ball and establish just how long a piece of lace is required to go all the way round and overlap by about ½" (1cm). Measure this length along the side of the pricking and mark the finishing line.

1. Kisses

4 pairs of Twilley's Gold Dust for passives. Cut 4 30" (75cm) lengths.
2 pairs of DMC Coton Perlé No 8 for workers. Cut 2 120" (300cm) lengths.

WORKING INSTRUCTIONS

Hang one pair of glittery passives on each of pins 2, 3, 4 & 5 for the cloth stitch trails at each side of the strip. Hang the perlé workers on pins 1 and 6. Twist the workers twice at the end of every row. To make the 'kiss' (marked with an X on the pattern, but with no pinhole) bring the workers to the inner edge of both trails, twist them twice and put up the pins as usual. Make a cloth stitch with the two workers then twist each worker pair twice before continuing in cloth stitch to the outside edge of each trail. The workers will therefore exchange sides each time they come to the centre. Complete the strip by repeating pins 11-16 as marked on the working diagram.

To finish, bring the workers to the inner edge of each trail, but don't twist them, put up the pin as usual. Now slip one of the worker threads underneath the pin and tie a reef knot around it. Tie each pair of passives with a reef knot and trim all the ends close to the knots.

As always when gluing the strip onto the ball start from the finishing end so that the neater starting end laps over and hides the knots of the finish. Spread the glue only along the two edge trails so that if you wish you can thread a ribbon through the slots formed by the kisses. Tie this in a nice bow to hide the overlap.

Right: Three Christmas Ball Decorations.

Top: Zigzag (No.3)
Middle: Kisses (No.1)
Lower: Chain (No.2)

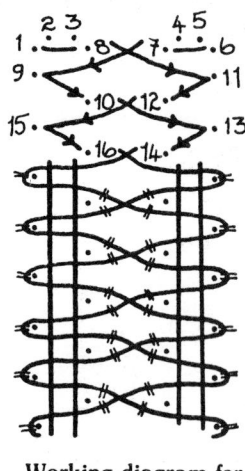

Working diagram for 'Kisses'

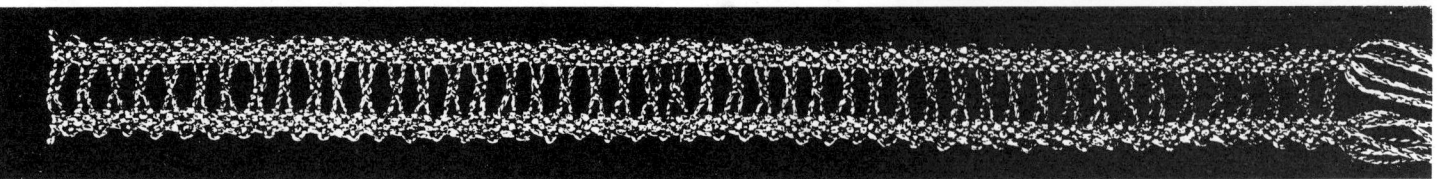

Below: Sample of finished lace 'Kisses'

Below: Pricking for 'Kisses'

54

2. Chain.

4 pairs of Twilley's Gold Dust as passives. Cut 4 36" (90cm) lengths.
2 pairs of DMC Coton Perlé No 8 as workers. Cut 2 120" (300cm) lengths.

To fit a ball with a 2¼" diameter you will need to work 9 ovals. It may not be possible to adapt this pattern very easily to fit a ball of a different size as it is vital that this pattern should match exactly at the join and it is quite a large pattern repeat. So check the measurements of the ball you intend to use very carefully before you embark on this pattern.

WORKING INSTRUCTIONS

There are two pairs of passives in each trail and it may help a less experienced worker to wind the two pairs of passives for one trail onto dark coloured bobbins and the two pairs for the other trail onto light coloured bobbins. This will be a useful guide when, at the end of each oval, the passives from each trail cloth stitch through each other to become the passives on the opposite side.

Hang one pair of glittery passives on each of pins 2, 3, 4 & 5. (If you are using distinctive coloured bobbins for the two different trails then the pairs on pins 2 & 3 should be the same and the pairs on pins 4 & 5 should be similar.) Cloth stitch the pair from 3 through the pairs from pins 4 & 5, then take the pair from pin 2 and cloth stitch it through the same two pairs. Now hang the workers on pins 1 & 6 and start cloth stitching to and fro across the trails following the markings on the pattern. Twist the workers twice at the end of every row.

Where the two workers make a diamond shape at the end of the oval the passives of the two trails will work through each other, so leave the two pairs of workers around pins A and B whilst you make the crossing. This crossing can be explained as the first half of a spider or by making 4 cloth stitches in the following order. First use the centre 4 glittery bobbins, then the group of four passives on the right followed by the group of four on the left. Finally use the centre four bobbins once more. If this has been done correctly the dark coloured bobbins of one trail will now make up the trail on the opposite side of the oval, and the light coloured bobbins will be all together in the second trail.

Finish with a trail crossing and tie reef knots with all the pairs. Trim the ends and glue the piece to the ball starting with the finishing end and lapping the starting end over the top. As you glue it onto the ball keep checking that the first crossing will lap neatly over the last, it is possible to stretch the chain a little to ensure that the join matches accurately.

3. Zig-zag.

3 pairs of DMC Fil a Dentelle passives. Cut 3 36" (90cm) lengths.
1 pair of Twilley's Gold Dust workers. Cut 1 90" (225cm) length.

WORKING INSTRUCTIONS

This is quite a simple piece consisting entirely of cloth stitch and twist, but the four pinholes around the inner curves are very close together and you must take care not to miss one and get out of step with the zig-zag. As with the preceding pattern you must check the length of lace required to go all the way round the ball you are using, and then see if this fits in with a whole number of repeats, because once again the pattern repeat is quite large and it is important for the patterns to match exactly at the join.

Hang the worker on pin 1 and one pair of passives on each of pins 2, 3 & 4. Work all across the row with a cloth stitch and twist (twisting both the worker and the passive). Add an extra twist to the workers at the end of every row, making a total of two twists around the pin.

Work down to the finishing line (this length of lace will go all the way round a 2¼" diameter ball and meet edge to edge without an overlap). Tie off each pair of bobbins with a reef knot and trim the ends. When gluing the piece to the ball keep checking that you are on target for the start to meet up exactly with the finishing edge, it is easy to stretch the zig-zag a little, or to ease the lace on to the ball to ensure an accurate join.

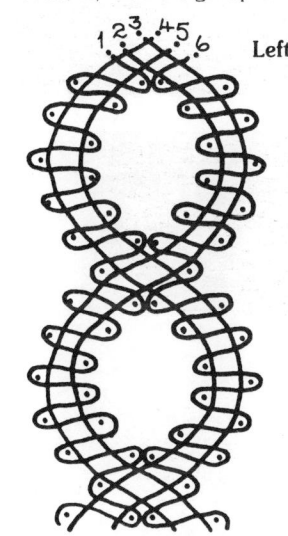

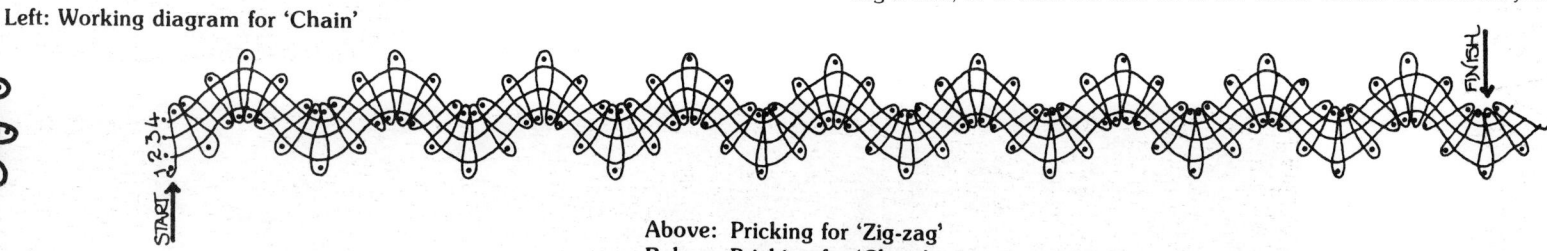

Left: Working diagram for 'Chain'

Above: Pricking for 'Zig-zag'
Below: Pricking for 'Chain'

4. Crosses.

4 pairs of Twilley's Gold Dust as passives. Cut 4 30" (75cm) lengths.
2 pairs of Twilley's Gold Dust for the crosses. Cut 2 40" (100cm) lengths.
2 pairs of DMC Coton Perlé No 8 for workers. Cut 2 100" (250cm) lengths.

WORKING INSTRUCTIONS

Hang the 4 shorter pairs of glittery passives from pins 2, 3, 6 & 7. Hang the two longer pairs of glittery threads from pins 4 & 5 and the workers from pins 1 & 8.

Take the worker pair from pin 1 and cloth stitch it through the two pairs of trail passives, twist the workers once and then cloth stitch them through the glittery pair from pin 4, twist the workers twice and put up pin 9. Cloth stitch back through the pair from pin 4, twist the workers once and then cloth stitch through the trail pairs, twist the workers twice because it is the end of the row and put up pin 10. Work pins 11 & 12 working through the two pairs of trail passives only. Leave the workers at pin 12 and return to the worker hanging from pin 8. Establish the trail on this side in exactly the same way, twisting the worker once before working through the pair from pin 5 on the way to pin 13, and working pins 14, 15 & 16 in the usual way remembering to twist the worker once after working through the pair from pin 5 on the way to pin 14.

Now make the 'cross' by taking the two centre pairs (originally from pins 4 & 5) and twisting each pair twice, now make a half stitch, pin, half stitch, putting up pin 17 in the centre. Twist each pair once more to give a total of two twists below the pin to balance with the two twists you put on above the pin before the half stitch.

The two 'cross' pairs now briefly re-join the trail at pins 18 & 22. The trail workers twist once before cloth stitching through a 'cross' pair, twice before putting up the pin, and then once again after working back through the 'cross' pair on the way to the edge pin. Repeat from pin 17 to pin 34 until the strip is long enough to fit the ball. Finish and mount in the usual way.

Right: Three Christmas Ball Decorations

Top: 'Criss-Cross' (No.5)
Middle: 'Loop the Loop' (No.6)
Bottom: 'Crosses' (No.4)

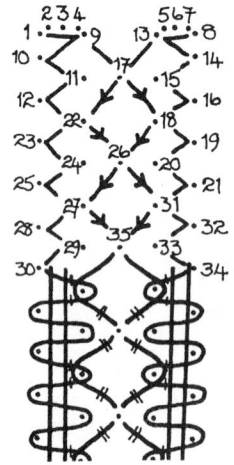

Left: Working diagram for 'Crosses'

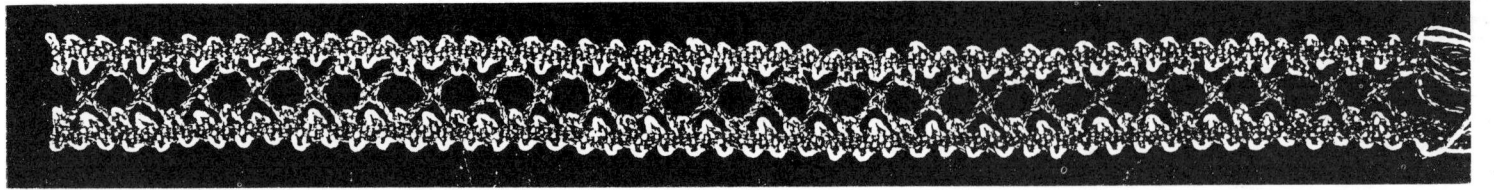

Above: Sample of finished lace 'Crosses'

Below: Pricking for 'Crosses'

5. Criss-Cross.

4 pairs of Twilley's Gold Dust as trail passives. Cut 4 30" (75cm) lengths.
2 pairs of Twilley's Gold Dust as 'criss-cross' passives in one colour.
2 pairs of Twilley's Gold Dust as 'criss-cross' passives in a contrasting colour.
Cut 4 40" (100cm) lengths for the 'criss-cross' passives.
2 pairs of DMC Coton Perlé No 8 as workers. Cut 2 100" (250cm) lengths.

WORKING INSTRUCTIONS

Using two contrasting colours for the centre 'criss-cross' section of this pattern can be very helpful, as if the stitches are made correctly you will find that the pattern forms diamonds in alternate colours.

Hang the shorter glittery passives from pins 2, 3, 7 & 8 for the edge trails. Hang two 'criss-cross' passives in the same colour from pins 4 & 6. Hang the other two pairs of passives in the contrasting colour from pin 5 and interlink them (hang the first pair around the pin and space the bobbins a little apart, hang the second pair around the same pin and place the right hand bobbin of the second pair to the right of the first pair, and the lefthand bobbin between the two bobbins of the first pair. Twist the two centre threads right over left). Now put one twist on both pairs hanging from pin 5.

Take the worker from pin 9 and cloth stitch through the two trail passives, twist it once before cloth stitching through the criss-cross pair from pin 6, twist the worker twice and put up pin 10, work back through the first passive and twist the workers once before completing the row with two twists at pin 11. Now take the criss-cross pair from pin 10, twist it once and make a half stitch with the right hand pair from pin 5, put up pin 12, and cover it with another half stitch. Bring the workers from pin 11 through the trail passives and twist them once, cloth stitch them through the righthand pair from pin 12, twist the workers twice and put up pin 13. Don't forget to twist the workers once after working back through the criss-cross passive towards pin 14.

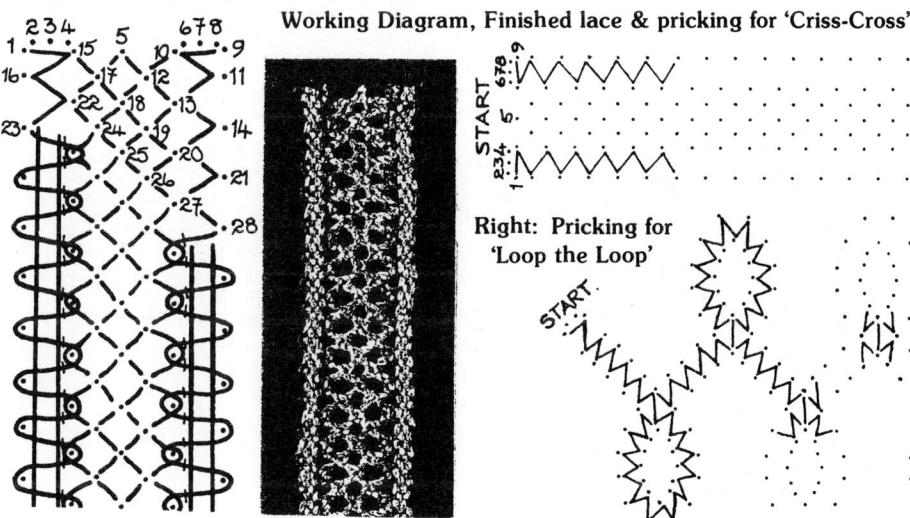

With the workers from pin 1 cloth stitch through the trail pairs, twist them once and work through the pair from pin 4, twist twice and put up pin 15, work back to pin 16 in the usual way. Twist the criss-cross pair from pin 4 once and work pins 17, 18 & 19 in a diagonal line, all are worked in half stitch, pin, half stitch. Take the righthand pair from pin 19 into the trail at pin 20, remembering to twist the worker before and after cloth stitching through it and to twist the criss-cross pair once as it leaves the trail. Keep working in these diagonal rows (follow pins 22-28) until you have completed the required length. Tie off in the usual way.

6. Loop the Loop.

2 pairs of Twilley's Gold Dust as passives. Cut 2 84" (210cm) lengths.
1 pair of DMC Fil a Dentelle workers. Cut 1 300" (750cm) length.

Although the lace in itself is not as difficult as some of the previous pieces, it is a considerably longer project and it does require two sewings at every trail crossing, so it is not for younger lacemakers!

Hang one pair of passives on each of the trail starting pins and the worker on the lefthand pin. Make a cloth stitch trail with two twists at the end of every row. You will need to turn your pillow as you work to ensure that you are always working your trail straight towards you. Four pinholes are used twice as the trail crosses the previously worked lace. Make a sewing into the first shared pinhole, simply use the previous pin in the usual way for the second and third shared pinholes and then make another sewing into the fourth. If you feel you would like more practice at sewings, then you can always make a sewing into all four!

You will need a length of eighteen loops to fit the 2¼" diameter ball. Make the sewings on the final crossing in the usual way, then knot and cut off each pair. Don't worry about the knots because the neater starting edge will lap over this part of the finish when you glue the lace to the ball. Take care to position the loops centrally and as always start with the finishing end.

Working Diagram, Finished lace & pricking for 'Criss-Cross'

Right: Pricking for 'Loop the Loop'

CHRISTMAS DECORATIONS IN RINGS.

All of the following patterns are worked in or around an inexpensive metal bangle. These are widely available on market stalls or in fancy goods shops. They are available in three sizes, the smallest is 2⅛" (5.5cm) in diameter, the medium one is 2⅜" (6cm) and the largest is 2⅝" (6.5cm). Most of my designs fit the medium sized ring, but it is possible to enlarge the pattern slightly in order to use the larger size. I have included prickings in both sizes so that you can use which ever one is closest in size to your rings. To check which size is best simply place the bracelet over the pricking, the outermost pins of the pricking should just touch the inner edge of the bangle.

1. Snowflake, Diamond and Flower.

All are made with a worker pair of Twilley's Gold Dust which forms the shape and 6 pairs of background threads which are very much finer. If you use fine green threads as the background passives they will simply appear to disappear when these decorations are hung on the Christmas tree and the shape of the snowflake, diamond or flower, will stand out very boldly!

6 pairs of DMC 30 Brilliant or DMC Fil a Dentelle. Cut 6 30" (75cm) lengths.
1 pair of Twilley's Gold Dust in either gold or silver.
    For the Snowflake cut 1 120" (300cm) length for the medium ring.
                        135" (335cm) length for the large ring.
    For the Flower cut 1 130" (325cm) length for the medium ring.
                       145" (365cm) length for the large ring.
    For the Diamond cut 1 90" (225cm) length for the medium ring.
                       100" (250cm) length for the large ring.

WORKING INSTRUCTIONS

The instructions for working all three are much the same, it's only the shape which varies. Firstly fold the worker thread in half and pass the loop under the edge of the bracelet, put the two ends of that thread over the bracelet and through the loop. Keeping the ends level pull the threads tight. Now look for the join in the bangle, if this is very apparent then slide the thread round the bracelet until it rests over the join. Place the ring centrally over the pricking which has been pinned to the middle of your pillow. Turn it until the thread is directly over the starting point of the design as indicated on the pricking, put a pin through the thread loop just inside the ring, now place two or three more pins inside the ring, spacing them evenly around the ring and pushing them tightly against it. Push these holding pins right down into the pillow so that the head presses down on the edge of the bangle and it is then securely anchored to both pattern and pillow.

Hang the 6 pairs of background threads on pins placed in the circled pinholes marked on the patterns. Every stitch you make will be a cloth stitch and twist (with one twist on both the worker and the passive background pair). Bring the workers through the first two background pairs following the working line which is marked on the pricking. Put an extra twist on the workers at the end of every row before putting up the pin in the usual way.

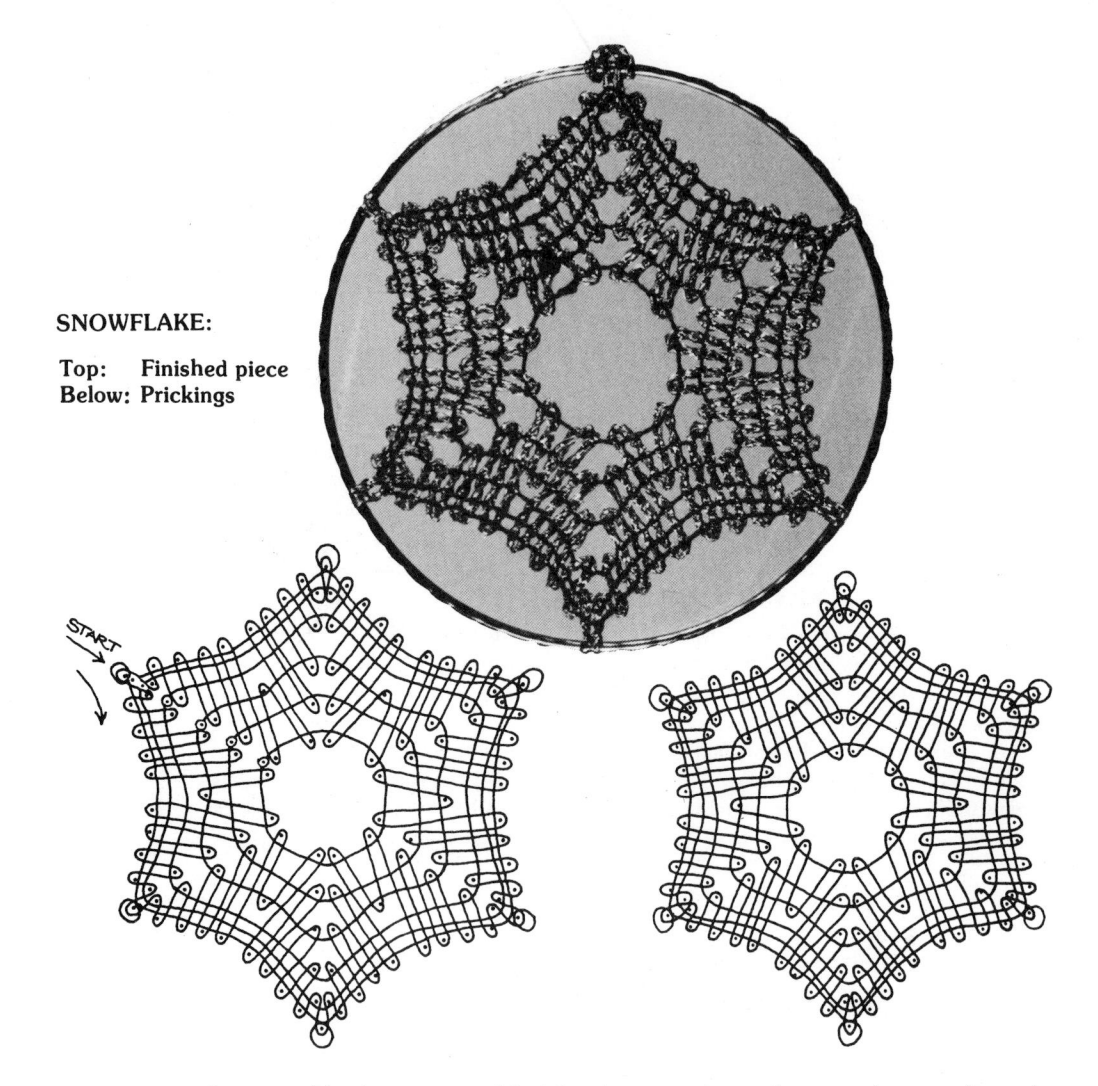

SNOWFLAKE:

Top: Finished piece
Below: Prickings

On some of the designs you will find that there is in places a larger gap between the worker threads, so to help the passives cross these larger spaces you can put extra twists on the background threads, a total of 2 or 3 twists should be quite adequate.

The number of background threads required for each row increases or decrease's nearly every time, so follow the markings on the pattern very carefully. Tensioning is tricky, but at the end of every row you must guide each background thread into a smooth even line above the pathway marked on the pattern.

Each time that the worker comes to one of the circled holes at the edge of the pattern you must link the worker to the ring. The snowflake is linked 6 times to the outer ring, the flower fives times and the diamond four. This is done by simply pushing the outer of your

FLOWER:

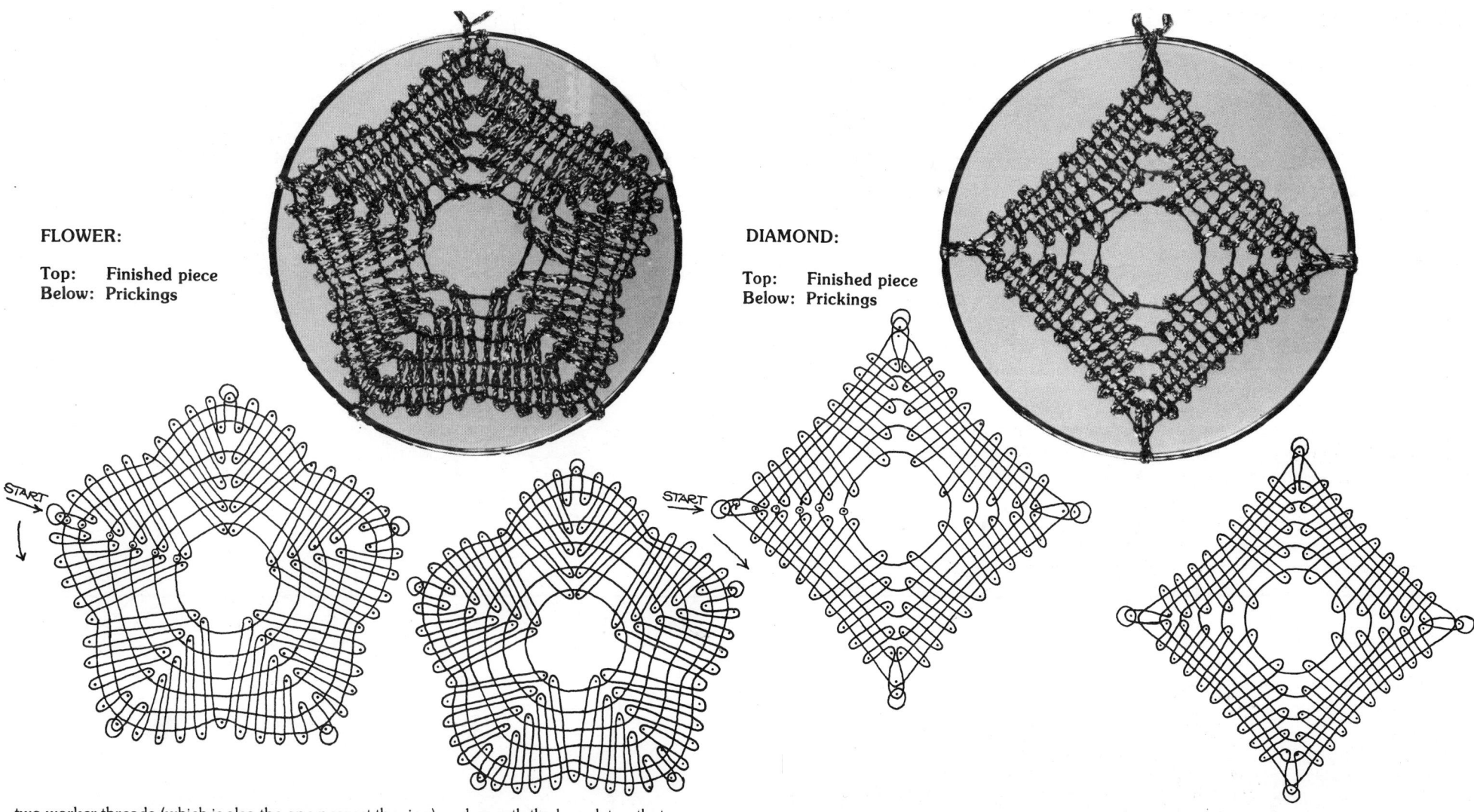

Top: Finished piece
Below: Prickings

DIAMOND:

Top: Finished piece
Below: Prickings

two worker threads (which is also the one nearest the ring) underneath the bracelet so that it forms a loop outside the ring. The bobbin does NOT go under the ring, it is just the thread which is pushed under, there should be no need to use a crochet hook, one of your lace pins, or even just your finger nail should be enough. Once you have the loop on the outside of the ring pass the OTHER worker bobbin through that loop, tighten both threads very carefully, twist them once and bring them back over the ring to continue the cloth stitch and twist sequence.

At the end the worker will return to the outer edge of the design and it will be tied around the bracelet and the worker thread at the starting point. Once each of the background threads has been tied securely into its corresponding starting loop (use a crochet hook to bring one thread of each pair through the correct starting loop and simply tie a reef knot) all the bobbins can be removed and the pins taken out. Now trim off the background threads, do NOT cut off the workers as having knotted them securely to the outside ring knot them together again about 2-3" (5-7cm) away from the bracelet and you will have made a loop with which to hang it from your Christmas tree. Trim off the surplus thread.

You can have great fun making these very inexpensive Christmas decorations, they are so quick and easy to do. You can try out various colour combinations, or for a different effect try twisting only the background threads and not the workers (except at the end of each row when they should be twisted twice as usual). They'll look beautiful hanging from your Christmas tree, mounted on a mobile or hanging in a window.

2. Zig-zag Circles.

Both of these designs use the same principle of one glittery worker pair and six darker background threads.

6 pairs of background passives in DMC Coton Perlé No 8 or DMC Fil a Dentelle or DMC 30 Brilliant. Cut 6 30" (75cm) lengths.
1 pair of Twilley's Gold Dust workers in the following lengths:
   For the 'Sun' 1 length of 96" (240cm).
   For the 'Zig-zag' 1 length of 72" (180cm).

For both patterns attach the worker thread to the ring in the way described for the previous ring decorations. Position the ring on the pattern and pin it down. Wind on the worker bobbins and set up the background threads in the holes marked on the pricking. Again the only stitch to be used is cloth stitch and twist (putting one twist on both the passive and worker pair) and twisting the worker once more at the end of every row to make a total of two twists before the pin. On all of these patterns you will need to put extra twists on some of the background passive pairs as the distance between the rows of workers increases. I have marked the suggested numbers of twists on the pricking. Every time the workers arrive at the outer edge of the pattern you must link them to the ring by pushing the outer worker thread (not the bobbin) underneath the bangle, then passing the other worker bobbin through the loop which has been created. Tension both threads, twist them once and continue the work.

At the end the workers will return to the edge of the ring and will be tied around the ring and the worker threads at the start, tie the workers again 2-3" (6-7cm) away from the ring to make the hanging loop. Each of the background passives must be tied off by bringing one thread of each pair through the appropriate starting loop and tying a reef knot. Trim off the ends & remove the pins.

As a finishing touch you might like to add a snowflake-shaped sequin to the centre of each circle, alternatively for a really eye-catching sparkle you could make a medium or a large sequin flower described in a later section, which is then glued into place.

You can also thread small beads onto the passive threads before you start, these are pushed into the work to form an eye-catching pattern. I used silver metal beads 2mm in diameter and slipped them into the work where the 2 rows of workers are positioned closest together in order to trap the beads tightly between one row and the next. You can also use small glass beads, in which case it is best to use beads of a contrasting colour to your main glittery workers, red beads with a green glittery worker look most effective. You can use larger beads, but if you do, you will not be able to position them on adjacent background threads, you will need to work out a pattern using them on alternate theads and possibly on the larger gaps between the workers rather than the smaller ones. Unless your beads are quite small it is best not to have any beads on the inner of the six pairs of background passives, the pinholes are quite close together here and it can become too crowded if you try to add beads as well. The size of the hole through the bead will determine which thread you will have to use for your background passives. You can use DMC Fil a Dentelle if the beads have a large hole, but you may have to use DMC 30 Brilliant if the holes are smaller.

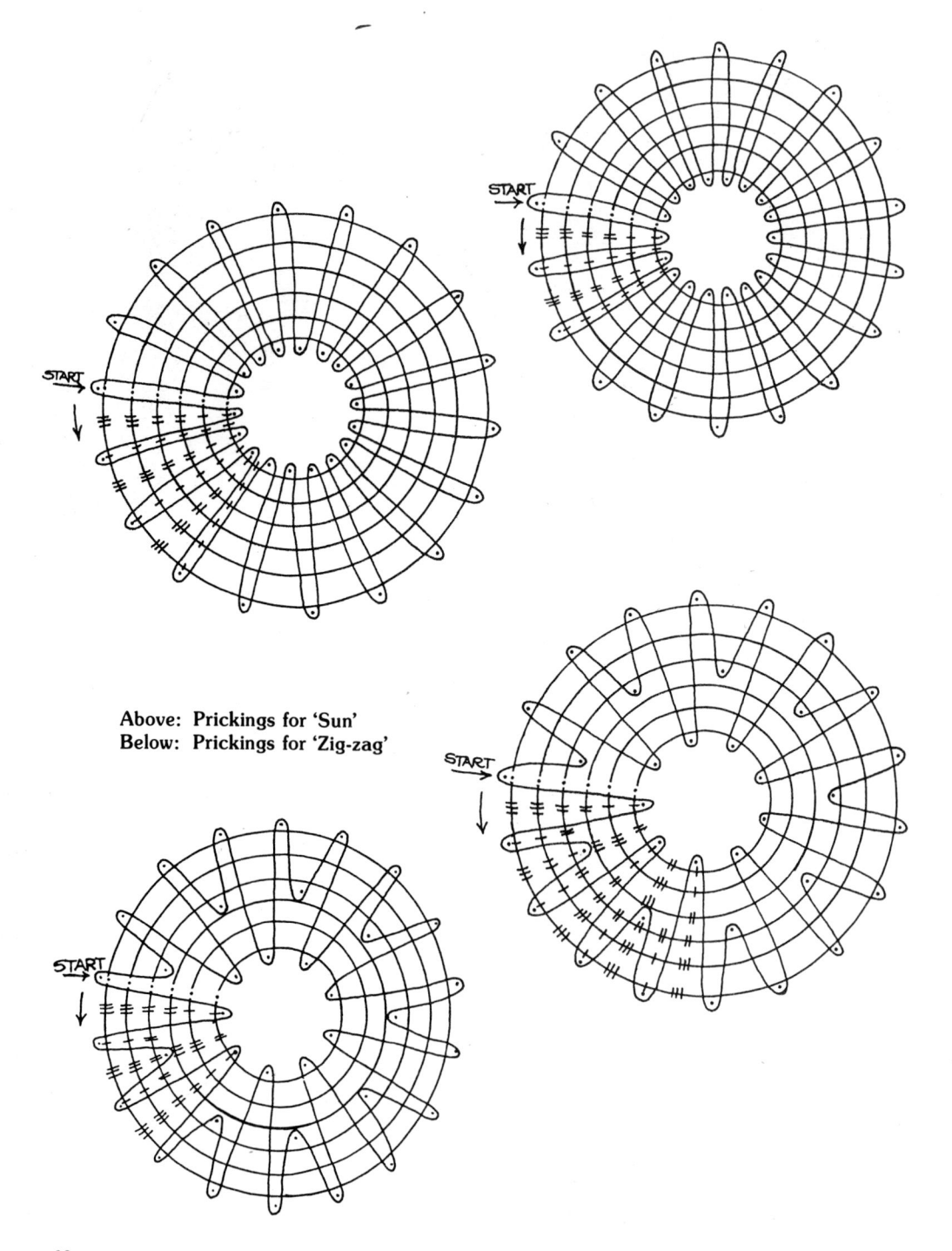

Above: Prickings for 'Sun'
Below: Prickings for 'Zig-zag'

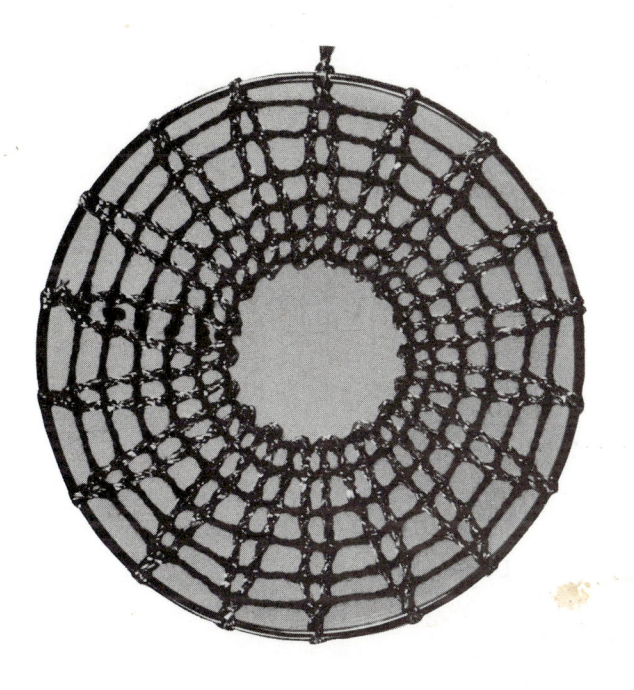

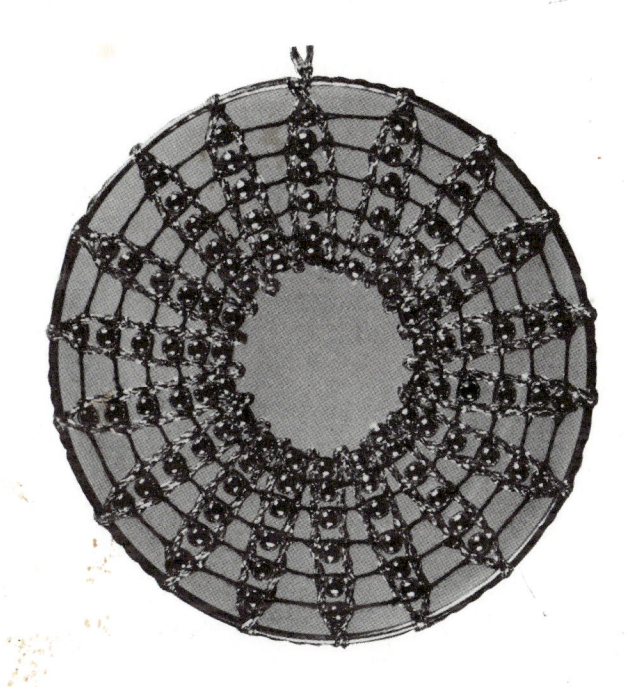

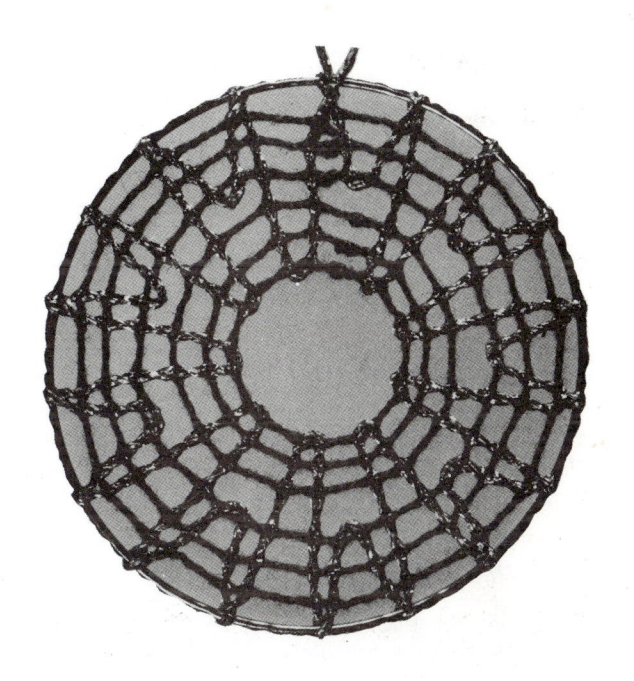

Wind half of the thread onto one bobbin as usual, then either you can thread the end of the length through a beading needle and thread the beads on, in the normal way, or you can use a lazy susan. With a lazy susan (a wooden handle into which a long, straight beading needle has been set with the eye facing outwards), just thread the beads onto the beading needle which has already been threaded with a contrasting coloured piece of cotton. You can put 9 or 10 beads on the needle at one time, then pull the coloured thread a bit looser just below the eye of the lazy susan and above the beads. Now pass the end of your lace thread through the space between the coloured thread & the beading needle, pull about 6" (15cm) of the lace thread through, then slide all the beads down the needle in the lazy susan and slip them onto the lace thread. You will need to count up how many beads will be needed and thread the appropriate number onto each pair. Wind the second bobbin as usual. If you have a large number of beads on any one pair then you will find that it is more convenient if you push half of the beads to each side of the starting pin (9 on each thread is less troublesome than 18 on one!).

There is no need to add extra twists before pushing a bead into the work as there is nothing to anchor these twists in place, so just leave on the one twist that is already there before slipping a bead into the work. I found that the beads sat more evenly if I pushed up a bead from the lefthand thread of every pair along one row, rather than having some beads from the left and some from the right. Should you run out of beads on one thread of a pair, then you can always adjust the number of twists on the next row. If you choose nice sparkly beads rather than those which are one solid colour, the effect will be really stunning.

Above Far Left: 'Sun'
Above: 'Sun' with beads
Above Right: 'Zig-zag'

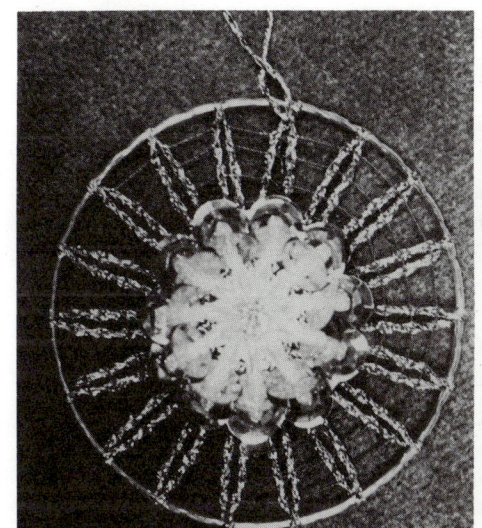

Finished Rings:

Lower Right: Zigzag with small sequin flower
Lower Left: 'Sun' with largest sequin flower

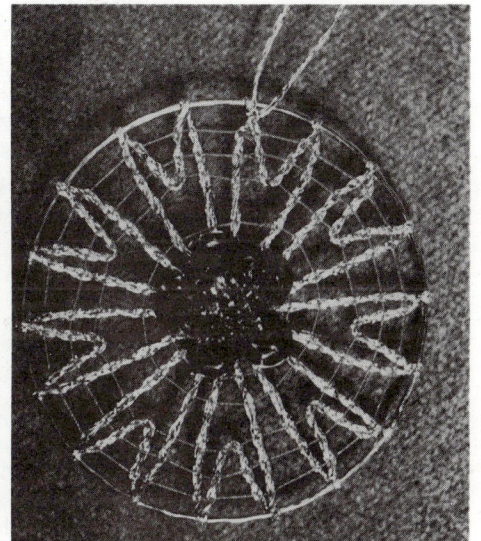

3. Daisy Rings.

The same pricking can be used to give you all sorts of different effects by simply varying the colours you use and the stitches where those colours cross.

4 pairs of Twilley's Gold Dust. Cut 4 36" (90cm) lengths.
1 pair of Twilley's Gold Dust for the inner circle passive. Cut 1 16" (40cm) length.

Start by attaching one of the longer passives to the ring in the usual way. As this will be the top of the design when it is hanging it is best to choose the most dominant of the colours you are working with to attach to the ring. Position the ring on the pricking so that this thread is at the outside starting point, pin the ring down securely and wind on the bobbins. Place starting pins where shown and hang on the pairs in the correct order if you are working with more than one colour.

Take the pair from the outer edge and twist it four times, now work it through the pair from the next starting pin and put up the crossing pin. The stitches which are used to make these crossings determine the direction in which the coloured threads will work. A half stitch, pin, half stitch will mean that the colours go straight through the crossing, continuing along the diagonal line of working, but a cloth stitch, pin, cloth stitch will mean that the colour is turned back on itself and will then return towards the outer ring producing a zig-zag effect. It is possible to use a combination of these two crossings in any one piece to produce a very interesting and colourful effect.

Twist the pair working towards the centre to make a total of three twists and work the second crossing pin with the pair hanging from the next starting pin. Make sure that the pair going towards the centre has been twisted twice in all and proceed to work the next crossing pin in the same way. Following that pin, the pair going towards the centre is only twisted once before cloth stitching through the innermost passive. Twist the 'worker' twice and put up the inner edge pin. Cloth stitch back through the inner ring passive & twist the 'worker' once more. Whatever stitches are used at the crossing pins the working on the innermost pins remains the same so that the same passive pair runs round in a circle without any twists at all. This completes the first diagonal row.

Now return to the outermost passive and make sure that it is twisted a total of four times, then link it to the bangle by pushing the nearest thread under the ring to make a loop. Push the other bobbin of this pair through that loop and tension both threads carefully. Put up the outermost pin as usual, twist the pair and bring them back into the ring below the pin to continue the work.

You are now ready to work the next diagonal row of crossing pins, remembering that the total number of twists on pairs between the crossing pins varies according to the distance between those pins, four twists on the outermost row, three on the next row, two on the next and just one on the innermost row.

At the end each pair will return to its own starting loop, the outer pair will be tied around the bangle and used to make the hanging loop, one thread of each of the other pairs will be brought through the corresponding starting loop, tied with a reef knot and cut off.

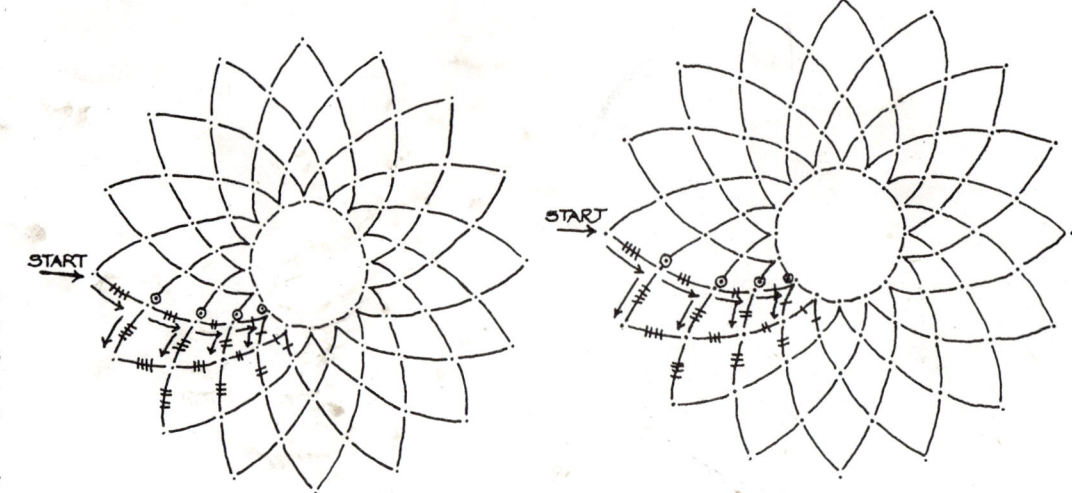

Prickings for Daisy Rings

Here are a few suggested colour combinations:-

Use five threads all of the same colour.

Choose two colours and cut two long passives in each colour. Cut the shorter passive in one or other of those colours. Hang the brighter colour from the ring and hang alternate coloured passives from the starting pins above the crossings. Work every crossing in half stitch, pin, half stitch.

Choose three colours eg. red, green and gold. Cut one long passive in each of the red and green, and two in gold. Join the red to the ring at the start, then hang on one gold passive, followed by one green and one gold. The centre ring passive is best done in gold. Work all the crossing pins in half stitch, pin, half stitch.

Choose four different colours and once again attach the brightest to the ring. Hang the other passives from the starting pins in the order which you prefer and work every crossing pin with a cloth stitch, pin, cloth stitch. This will create 4 rows of zig-zags, each in a different colour. The inner passive ring can be worked in any of the colours although it will look best if it matches the innermost zig-zag row.

Choose two colours and cut two long lengths in silver for example, for the outer zig-zag rows; the innermost ring passive and two shorter lengths for the two inner zig-zag rows in green. Attach one of the silver threads to the ring and hang the other silver thread from the first crossing pin. The longer green threads will hang from the second and third crossing pins. The first and third row of crossing pins can be worked in half stitch, pin, half stitch, as each colour can continue in straight lines here, but the second row, where the two different colours come together must be worked in cloth stitch, pin, cloth stitch.

N.B. Add extra length to the outer passives if you are going to use the cloth stitch crossings as these will require a little more thread.

Templates for backing shapes of sequin flowers

Templates for tinsel circles

Daisy Rings:
Top Left: Half stitch crossings throughout
Right: Cloth stitch crossings throughout
Left: Alternate half-stitch & cloth-stitch crossings

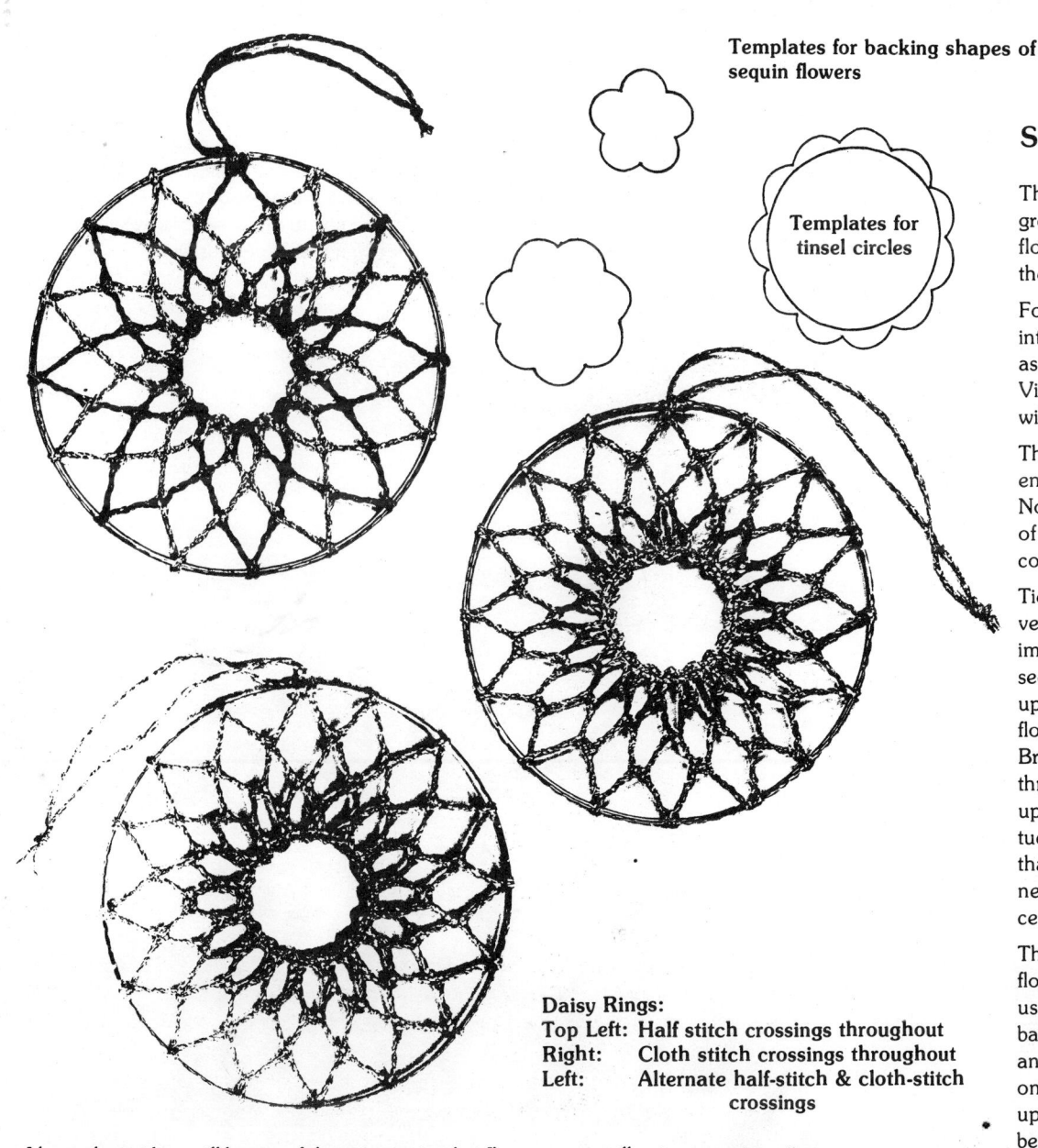

I hope these ideas will be a useful starting point, but I'm sure you will enjoy experimenting with your own colour schemes once you have got the idea of controlling the colour by varying the crossing stitches.

If you wish to add further decoration to these rings you can use a snowflake-shaped sequin or a flower made out of sequins attached to the centre.

SEQUIN FLOWERS.

These can be purchased commercially, but in a limited range of colours, you can have a great deal of fun working out your own colour combinations. The two larger sizes of flowers can be added to the centre of many of the Christmas decorations as well as using the smallest ones as the centres of the hair slide ornaments.

For the smallest flower cut out the five petalled backing shape in thick Vilene (non-woven interfacing for dressmaking). Trace the shape onto the Vilene and cut it out as accurately as you can. If your Vilene is not stiff enough then use a double thickness of Iron-on Vilene, which you have bonded together, or glue your shape to some paper-backed tinsel with Copydex and cut it out when it is dry.

Thread a fine needle with a double length of cotton, checking that the needle is fine enough to go through the tiny beads you will be using. Use a beading needle if necessary. Now select your sequins, ten 8mm cup-shaped sequins are required for the smallest size of flower, and you can use two colours if you wish. The small beads can either match or contrast with the colour of the sequins.

Tie a knot in the end of your cotton and bring the needle out in the centre of one petal, very close to the outer edge. Thread on the first sequin upside down (this is very important, the flower will not be satisfactory if you don't get this right). After the first sequin, thread on one bead followed by a sequin the correct way up (ie. edges curving upwards towards you), and two more beads. Now stitch down through the middle of the flower shape and pull the thread tight making sure that the sequins are eased into place. Bring the needle out at the edge of the next petal and repeat the sequence, going down through exactly the same centre hole as you made last time. The background layer of upside down sequins will not overlap, but the inner ones which form the flower need to be tucked behind the edge of the previous one in a regular way each time. This will ensure that one edge of each sequin will be visible rather than two edges of one and neither of the next. If you wish you can sew another small bead, perhaps of a different colour, into the centre to finish it off.

The larger seven petalled flower can be made in exactly the same way, but the largest flower of all is a little more complex. The backing shape is cut out in the same way as usual, but this time it is essential to cover the front with a circle of silver or gold paper-backed tinsel glued in place with Copydex. Use a long length of doubled sewing cotton and bring the needle through at the edge of the first petal. Again thread the first sequin onto your needle upside down, add one small bead followed by a sequin the correct way up, add two small beads and another sequin again the correct way up, now add two tiny beads and then a longer, oval-shaped bead before stitching down through the backing. This time do not go into the centre of the flower, but about 1/10" (2mm) short of the centre. Repeat this 10 more times and marvel at how easily the flower takes shape. You can add a larger bead or sequin (6mm) to the very centre at the end. Fasten your thread off and then cut another circle of foil to glue to the back so that the stitching will be hidden when you attach it to your Christmas decoration.

4. Half Stitch Circle with Sequins.

The pattern for this piece has been drawn to fit the smallest sized ring (5.5cm in diameter).

5 pairs of Twilley's Gold Dust. Cut 5 48" (120cm) lengths.
1 pair of Twilley's Gold Dust in a different colour. Cut 1 30" (75cm) length.

Take one of the main coloured threads and attach it to the ring in the usual way, secure the ring to the pillow and wind on the bobbins. Hang the differently coloured pair from the lefthand-most starting pin, and one pair from each of the other starting pins. The pair which is attached to the ring starts off as the 'workers' and makes a double half stitch (or cloth stitch and twist) with the passive pair at the outer edge. Now half stitch across the row putting an extra two twists on the workers at the end of every row (which will make a total of three twists altogether). Tension all the pairs well after putting up the pin.

Continue in the same way taking care to work that double half stitch with the contrasting coloured edge passives. This will ensure that they stay as the outlining pair at the edge of the scallop. If you find that they are not on the outside at any point, then you must look for an error!

Link the worker pair to the ring at the circled edge pinholes by pushing the nearest worker thread (not bobbin) underneath the ring to make a loop. Pass the other worker bobbin through that loop & pull tight. Put up the edge pin in the usual way and continue working.

The pinholes at the inner edge are quite close, so make sure that you do not miss any out and get out of step with the zig-zag marking on the pricking.

At the end the worker returns to the edge and is tied onto the bracelet and starting thread, tie another knot 2-3" (6-7cm) away from the ring to make the hanging loop. One thread of every pair is brought through the corresponding starting loop and tied with a reef knot. Remove all the pins and trim off all the ends.

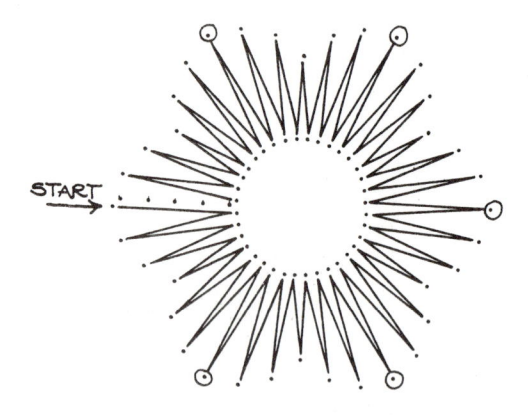

Pricking for half stitch circle

Take a needle which is fine enough to go through the small glass beads which will be sewn to the centre of each flower-shaped sequin, and thread it with some fine thread which matches the background colour of your lace. Thread the sequin and then the bead onto your needle and return through the centre hole of the sequin, now thread another sequin and bead onto your needle and stitch both in place exactly behind the first. Run the needle along through the lace until you reach the widest point of the next scallop and repeat the process. You can choose to alternate the colour of the sequins and even put a completely different colour combination on the reverse side of your work!

Finished half stitch circle decorated with flower-shaped sequins

5. Ring with Bell.

2 pairs of Twilley's Gold Dust as passives. Cut 2 36" (90cm) lengths.
1 pair of Mez Effektgarn or DMC Fil a Dentelle workers. Cut 1 110" (275cm) length.

This pattern is designed to go round the edge of the smallest sized bracelet (5.5cm in diameter).

Attach one of the glittery passives at its mid-point to the ring in the usual way, secure the ring to the centre of the pricking and wind on the bobbins. Hang the worker from its pinhole on the left at the deepest point of the V and the remaining passive from a pin placed between the worker and the ring.

There is only one sequence of stitches — cloth stitch and two twists on the workers. Do not twist the passives here at all. The workers twist at the end and in the middle of every row to separate the two passive pairs. Tension each row carefully to make sure that the passives lie smoothly. At the inner V of every scallop, whilst the workers wait around the outer edge pin, link the inner passives to the ring by pushing the nearer thread underneath the bangle to form a loop. Pass the other passive bobbin through that loop, and tension

Left: Finished rings, one trimmed with holly leaves & ribbon bow, the other with leaves & berries

both threads carefully. Twist the threads once and bring them back to the outside of the ring to continue the work. If you put up a pin now, close to the bracelet and just below the threads which linked the work to the ring, it will prevent these threads from sliding out of position.

At the end bring one of the worker threads through its own starting loop and tie a reef knot with an extra twist on the first half. The outer passive can be finished off in the same way, alternatively tie a reef knot with the threads and trim off the ends (it doesn't have to be fastened to its starting loop as two holly leaves will shortly be glued over it all). Take off the inner passive bobbins and remove the pins. Now thread one of the inner passive threads between the ring and the righthand scallop and the other between the ring and lefthand scallop, turn it over and tie a reef knot to secure it around the starting loop.

Using a crochet hook or a lazy susan pull both of the threads through the hole in the top of the silver or gold bell, now you need to enlist the help of a friend who can hold the threads and twist them as tightly as possible. Hold the threads firmly and slide the bell about an inch or so down the twisted threads, now fold the threads back up and catch them under your thumb where they cross the bracelet. Let go of the bell and the threads will twist into a nice cord. Untwist the surplus cord making sure to keep the twisted part securely under your thumb, now pass one of those threads between the bracelet and the righthand scallop and the other between the ring and the lefthand scallop, turn it over and tie a reef knot to secure the ends and the twists. Tie the threads together again about 2-3" (6-7cm) away from the ring to make the hanging loop. Trim off the ends.

Take two small gold or silver leaves and glue them (using gum or Copydex) to matching paper-backed tinsel. Let them dry well before trimming off the surplus. Snip off the wire from the leaves and gluing the two scallops on each side of the join press the leaves onto one side of the ring to cover the join in your lace. It looks best if you bring the leaves down into the ring a little. To add the finishing touch make a bow out of ribbon and glue it on top of the leaves, or use a small commercial embroidered motif on which the red flowers could be mistaken for holly berries! Make sure that you keep the hanging loop well clear of all the glue.

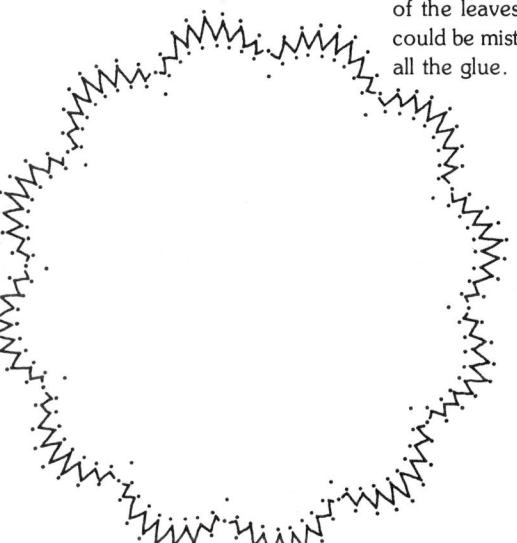

Pricking & Working Diagram for Ring with Bell

ANGELS FOR YOUR CHRISTMAS TREE

I have designed two sizes of angels, the smaller ones will hang nicely on the lower branches of the tree whilst the larger angel sits proudly on top of the highest point. Both are made out of cone-shapes, a larger one for the body/skirt (which is lined with card) and two smaller ones for the sleeves. The brightly coloured, shiny covering for all of the angels is paper-backed foil, which gives a lovely glittery surface, but which does present some problems when used with glue. Despite the paper backing most foil is adversely affected when chemical glues such as Bostik or Uhu are applied, so wherever possible it is best to use a paper gum, Copydex, or a similar craft glue. However most of these do not seem to have the same strength as the chemical glues and using them for some processes is unavoidable. Whenever they have to be used you must do so with great care applying the smallest possible quantity so that the surplus does not ooze out to where it will show, because wherever it touches it will remove the foil surface. You must also avoid touching your angel with gluey fingers for the same reason.

If you are planning to make more than one angel it is well worth the time to make card templates which can quickly and easily be drawn round time after time. I have given you the outlines for four templates for the smaller angel, one for the skirt, one to help you mark the skirt overlap, one for the sleeve and again one with which to mark the overlap. There are two sleeve templates for the larger angel, but you will only need one skirt template as the position of the overlap is determined by the pattern repeats of your lace.

Firstly cut out a semi-circle of card for the skirt, and using a child's paint brush spread gum over the entire surface. Press it down onto a larger piece of paper-backed foil and leave it to dry. Mark the skirt overlap onto the card semicircle for the smaller angel only. Trim the foil flush with the card all around the curved edge and halfway along the length of the straight side which is furthest away from the overlap line. Trim the remainder of that straight edge to within 1/8 (3mm) of the card. Taper this to nothing at the centre point of the straight edge.

Below: Small Angel with Zig-Zag French Fan skirt trim

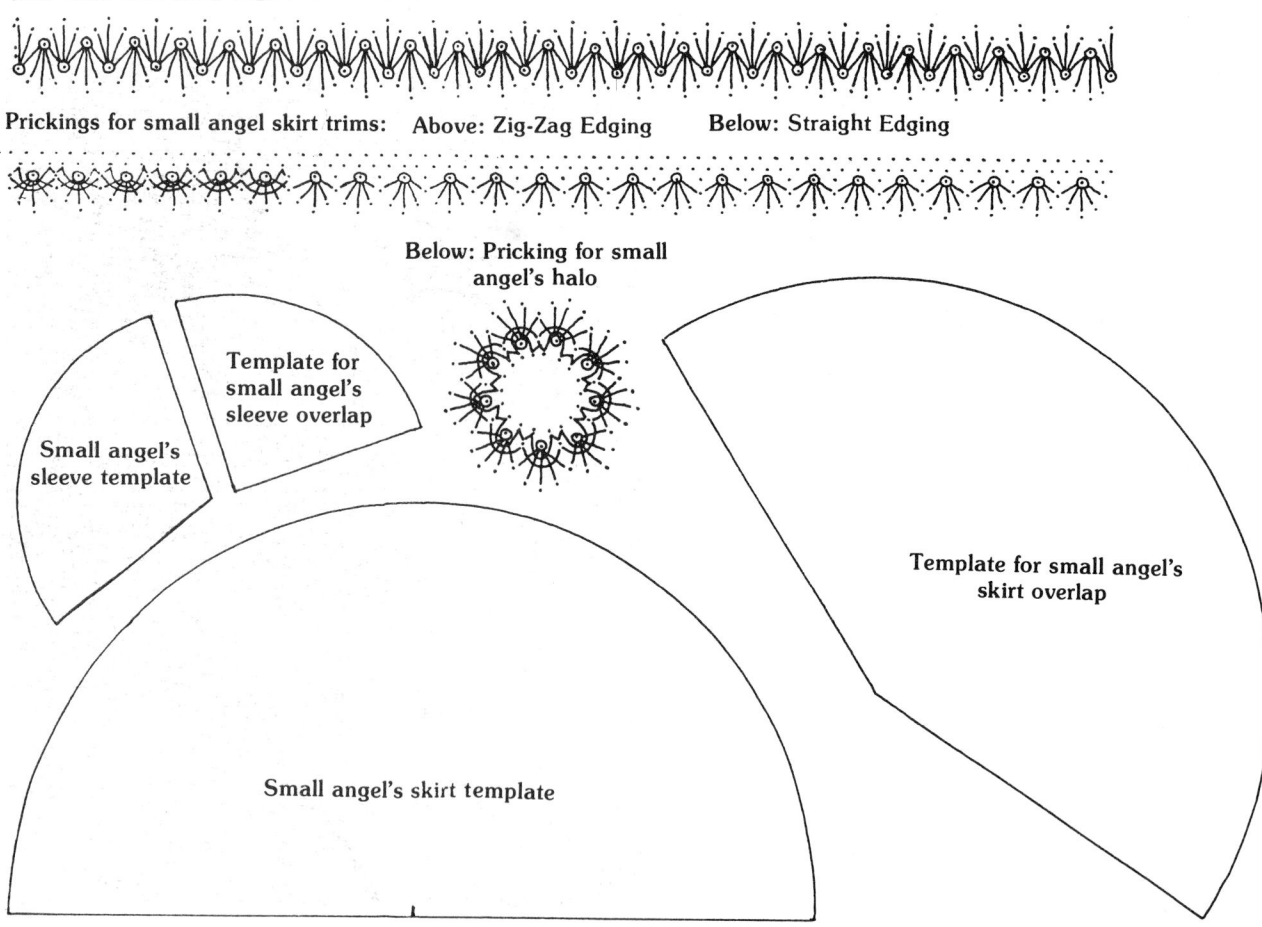

Prickings for small angel skirt trims: **Above: Zig-Zag Edging**   **Below: Straight Edging**

Below: Pricking for small angel's halo

Small angel's sleeve template

Template for small angel's sleeve overlap

Template for small angel's skirt overlap

Small angel's skirt template

66

Pricking for large angel's torchon skirt trim

Template for large angel's sleeve overlap

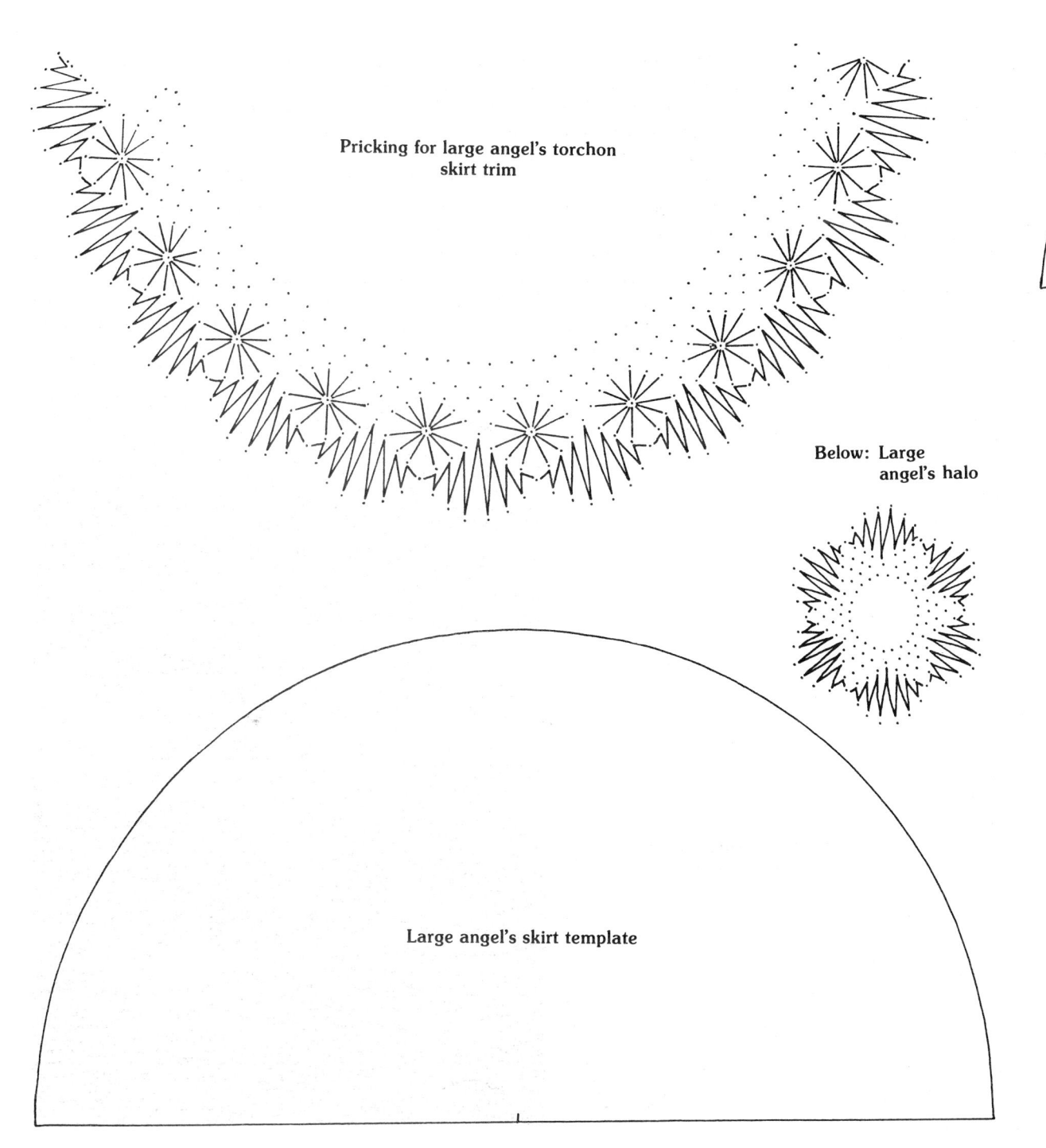

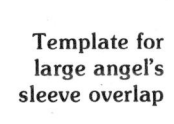

Large angel's sleeve template

Below: Large angel's halo

Below: Large Angel

Large angel's skirt template

From the same tinsel cut out two sleeve shapes using the larger template. Use the smaller template to mark on the overlap lines, measuring from the lefthand straight edge on one and from the righthand edge for the other. Using Bostik very sparingly form the sleeve cone matching the edge and the overlap line as accurately as possible. To fix the overlap firmly in place push the point of a pencil into the cone shape underneath the join and press against it.

For the larger angel only, you now glue the lace edging onto the skirt. To do this most efficiently use very small amounts of Bostik behind the footside trail and the solid area of the fans. Start by gluing the neater starting end to the straight edge which has the extra overlap of foil. Half of the fan will project beyond the edge of the foil, the start of the ground and footside trail should be lined up level with the edge. Glue a small section at a time and position the lace so that the edge of the fan is a constant distance from the lower edge of the skirt. The lace will not go all the way to the other end of the skirt, but it will go far enough to give you an overlap of about half a pattern.

Now form the skirt into the cone shape. This is easier if you make a small fold or nail mark just at the mid-point of the straight edge. For the smaller angel overlap the edge with the extra foil until the other edge meets the overlap line marked on the inside of the skirt. The larger angel proceeds in the same way, but the overlap is increased until the starting edge of the lace exactly matches the lace underneath it (the last and the first fan will now overlap completely). Glue the overlap of both angels with Bostik and hold until the glue is sufficiently set to maintain the shape. You can now add the lace to the skirt of the smaller angel. Glue down the starting end first and continue to glue down a small section at a time. Simply cut the lace to the required length and glue the final section in place (it is possible to stretch or ease the length of both of these skirt trimmings to match the pattern quite well).

To add the sleeves turn the skirt until the line of the overlap is exactly down the centre back, then apply a thin line of Bostik to the join line on the outside of the sleeve. Press it into place at the side of the angel with the points of the sleeve and skirt cones level. You can press the sleeves more firmly into place by using the pointed end of a pencil inserted into the cone.

Now you are ready to make the head. I used a pressed paper ball rather than a polystyrene one, and your first task is to enlarge the hole by pushing it onto the point of your pencil so that it will fit more easily over the combined points of the sleeves and skirt cones. If you wish to make a face on the angel then it is best to do it now before the head is fixed to the body. Experiment with various features and expressions before drawing them in pencil onto the ball. I used a fine rapidograph pen to ink in the very stylised face, let this dry really well before rubbing out any pencil which might still be showing. If you aren't happy with your first efforts, then turn the head round a bit and try again, her curls will cover your mistakes! It is also wise to test whichever pen and ink you will be using on part of the head where it will not show to make sure that the ink is not going to run - your angel is better without a face than with a blurred one! Simplistic, stylised features I found looked better than realistic or glamorous ones. Hair can be added if you wish. I used 'Chic' terry-look Double Knitting yarn by Robin in a pale primrose colour, but you could use any nubbly looking yarn to achieve a similar effect. Use 6 or so 3" (7.5cm) lengths of yarn and tie them into a bunch with a loop around the middle. Glue the centre to the angel's forehead and then spreading more glue over the head press the ends of the yarn down to give a smooth edge on each side of her face. Trim off any surplus curls, the loops of the yarn will hide a multitude of sins or inexperience, so don't worry if you don't achieve a perfect hair-do, the overall effect will still be one of angelic, yellow curls!

To fix the head in place take the tips of all three cones and pinch the top 1/8" (3mm) or so together with your thumb nail. Now fill the enlarged hole in the head with a generous amount of Bostik and press the head firmly into place. Hold it until the position is firm.

Next add the halo. With the larger angel you can either glue the ring of lace directly into place, or you can mount it onto a small circle of foil to match the skirt of the angel. This looks particularly attractive if you have used red or green foil for the skirt. To do this cut a circle of foil which is just a little larger than the central hole of the halo, glue this down onto a second piece of foil with gum or Copydex and trim round the edges when dry (to give you a foil surface on both sides of the circle). Using Bostik extremely sparingly touch the glue all round the inner edge of the halo and put it down on top of the circle of prepared foil. Press the edges down well. Now place the halo behind the angel's head so that a flattering amount of lace and foil shows above her hair. You can tilt it slightly forward if you like. Glue it into place putting Bostik on the lower part of the halo only.

The gold or silver wings are purchased from a craft shop. The smaller ones are double sided, but the larger ones need to have a second pair glued to the back of the first (alternatively you can back them with gold tinsel, or you can paint them gold). Position the wings, bending them slightly so that they follow the shape of the cone to give a good contact area for the glue (the smaller wings also have a hanging loop and this has to be bent back to accommodate the head and halo). For a nicer shape you can encourage the wing tips to curve slightly backwards. Glue in place with Bostik.

Complete the smaller angel by adding a hanging loop of glittery thread. I found that when suspended from that loop my angel tilted forward, so to restore her balance I selotaped a penny to the inside of the back of her skirt. If there are small children to whom this might be a hazard, then add a small ball of Blu-tack to give extra weight.

Large Angel's Skirt Trim.

A straightforward piece of torchon consisting of fans, spiders, torchon ground and a footside edge.

12 pairs of DMC 80 Cordonnet Special. Cut 12 1½ yard (150cm) lengths.
 1 pair of Twilley's Gold Dust for the fan workers. Cut 1 4½ yard (4.25cm) length. To accommodate 2¼ yards of this thread on a bobbin you will need to choose bobbins with an especially large thread capacity.

Hang one of the passive pairs onto pin 1, hang the glittery workers onto the same pin and interlink the threads by putting the second pair of bobbins down to the right of the first pair, now simply twist the centre two bobbins twice (right over left as usual). Hang one pair on each of pins T1, T2, T3, & T4. Now you can work the cloth stitch fan (pins 2-15) twisting the worker twice at the end of each row, Take four pairs and hang two pairs on each of pins 16 and 17. Interlink them as described above and twist each pair twice. Take the righthand pair from pin 16 and the lefthand pair from pin 17 and work a torchon ground stitch (half stitch, pin, half stitch and twist) at pin 18. Hang 2 more pairs from T5 and one from T6. Take the righthand pair from pin 17 and cloth stitch it through the two pairs from T5, twist the workers twice and cloth stitch them through the pair from T6. Twist both pairs twice and put up pin 19 inside both pairs (between the 2 working pairs and the two pairs of passives hanging from pin T5). Leave the pair from pin 17 at the edge and return with the pair from T6 as the workers. Cloth stitch through the footside trail, twist them twice and make a torchon ground stitch with the righthand pair from pin 18, put up pin 20. Work back through the footside passives and make up the footside by twisting the worker pair twice before cloth stitching it through the edge pair and putting up pin 21 two pairs in from the edge. Take the inner of the two pairs and work back across the footside trail. Work torchon ground stitches at pins 22-25 inclusive, make up footside pin 26. Work the spider around pin 27 making sure that each leg is twisted three times before working the body and three times afterwards. Complete the area of torchon ground at pins 28-33, 35, 36 & 38, making up the footside as you go with pins 34, 37 & 39. Work the next fan (pins 40-53), complete the torchon ground of pins 54-57 and the footside pin 58. Repeat from pin 27-58 inclusive until the strip is complete. Tie off each pair after the final fan and the spider body.

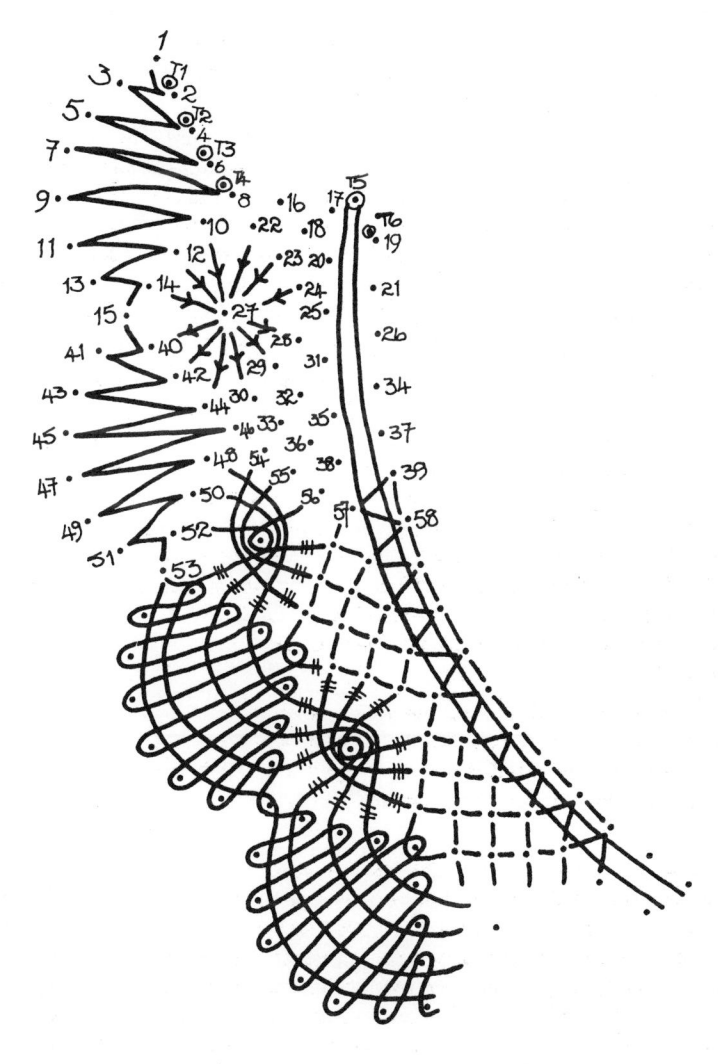

Finished lace for large angel's skirt trim

Above: Working diagram for large angel's torchon skirt trim

Small Angel's Skirt Trim.

1. Straight Edging with a French Fan.

4 pairs of Mez Effektgarn or similar fine metallic or glittery thread as passives and one as the trail worker. Cut 4 72" (200cm) lengths.
2 pairs of the same thread as passives for the trail. Cut 2 36" (100cm) lengths.
1 pair of the same thread as workers. Cut 1 144" (400cm) length.

Hang a pair of passives on T1, hang the workers from the same pin and put them down to the right of the first pair. Now twist the centre two bobbins twice (right over left as usual). Twist the outer passive once and the worker pair twice. Hang 2 passives from pin T2, interlink them in the same way and twist both pairs once more. Hang the two shorter passive pairs on T3 and the trail worker on T4. Cloth stitch the workers from T4 through the passives from T3 and the righthand pair from T2, twist the workers twice and put up pin 5, cloth stitch back to pin 6, twist twice and put up a pin. Take the pair from T2 which you have just cloth stitched through twice and twist it once. You are now ready to start the fan.

Take the worker from T1 and cloth stitch it through the two pairs to its right (both originally from pin T2), twist the workers twice and put up pin 7. Cloth stitch back to the outer edge of the fan always remembering to put two twists on the worker before cloth stitching through the outside passive which is then twisted once. The worker is always twisted twice at the end of every row. Work to and fro using pin 7 three more times in order to work pins 8, 9, 10 & 11. To use pin 7 as a pivot pin simply twist the workers as usual and lift the workers so that the thread goes around the back of the pin which is not removed at any time. Leaving the workers at pin 11 go back to the two inner passives of the fan and twist them each once.

Resume the edge trail working pins 12 & 13 as usual. At pin 14 work through the innermost passive pair from the fan and then cloth stitch back to pin 15. Take the inner pair which briefly joined the trail and twist it once and make a half stitch with the second inner passive from the fan, put up pin 16 and cover it with another half stitch. Take the trail workers through the two pairs of passives and the righthand pair from pin 16, twist twice and put up pin 17. Work back to pin 18. Take the pair which went into the trail and came straight out again and twist them once. You are now ready to start the fan again. Repeat pins 6-17 until you have completed 22 fans which will be plenty to go round the small angel's skirt.

2. Zig-Zag Edging with a French Fan.

3 pairs of Mez Effektgarn or similar fine metallic or glittery thread as passives. Cut 3 2 yard (200cm) lengths.
1 pair of the same thread as workers. Cut 1 6 yard (6m) length.

Hang the worker on T1 and one each of the passives on T2, T3 & T4. Cloth stitch straight through the pairs from T2 & T3, then twist the workers twice, cloth stitch through the pair from T4, twist the passive once and the worker twice, put up pin 5. Work back to pin T1 twisting the outside passive once, the worker twice between the inside and the outer passive, and twice again at the end of the row. Work to and fro in this way using pin T1 several times over without removing it, until the workers reach pin 7. Before you work back to pin 8 put one twist on the pair that was the innermost passive of the fan, this is now the outer passive, and the two passive pairs closest to pin 7 are the untwisted inner passives until you reach pin 11 when again the pivot pin changes as do the innermost and outermost passives.

Work the length of the pattern shown to give you 22 pairs of fans to go round the skirt of the small angel.

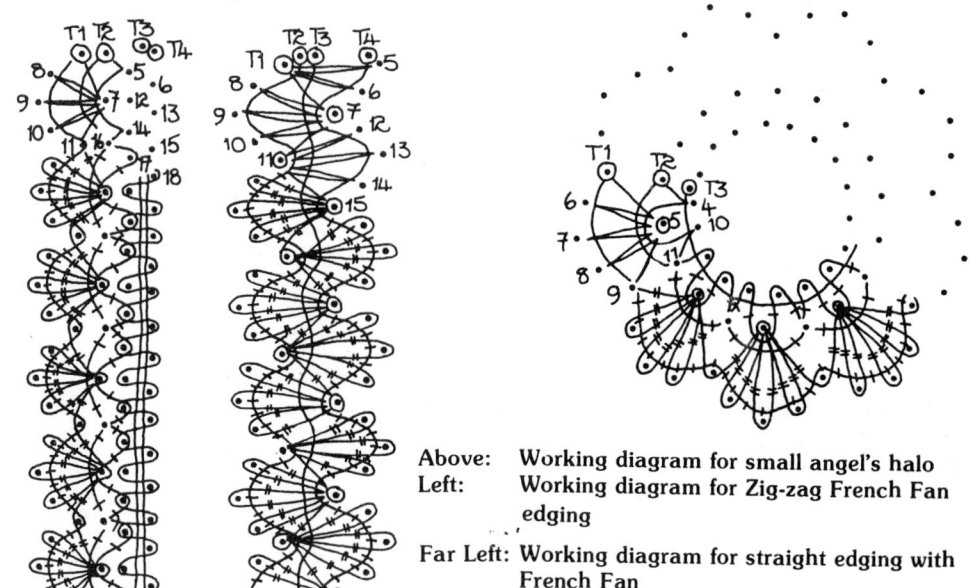

Above: Working diagram for small angel's halo
Left: Working diagram for Zig-zag French Fan edging
Far Left: Working diagram for straight edging with French Fan

Small Angel's Halo.

3 pairs of Mez Effektgarn or similar fine metallic or glittery thread as passives. Cut 3 36" (100cm) lengths.
1 pair of the same thread as workers. Cut 1 72" (200cm) length.
1 pair of the same thread as inner passives. Cut 1 24" (60cm) length.

Hang one of the passives on T1 and then the worker on the same pin. Interlink them as described on the straight edging and twist the passive once and the worker twice. Hang 2 pairs from T2 and interlink them and twist each pair once. Hang the shortest pair of passives from T3. Take the righthand pair from T2 and cloth stitch through the inner passive from T3, twist the workers twice and put up pin 4, work back and twist the workers once. Do not twist the inner passive at all. Go back to the worker at pin 1, cloth stitch through the two pairs of passives to its right and twist it twice, put up pin 5 which is the pivot pin for this fan. Complete the fan in the usual way and leave the worker outside pin 9. Twist both of the inner pairs of passives from the fan once, take the righthand one and cloth stitch it through the inner passives, twist it twice, put up pin 10 and work back again twisting it once before making a half stitch, pin, half stitch with the other inner fan passive pair at pin 11. You are now ready to work the next fan.

Work the 9 fans required to complete the circle and then continue working for two or three more pinholes to form a small overlap, tie off each pair with a reef knot and trim all the ends. Remove the pins and glue the overlap together. This will be the centre back of your halo.

Large Angel's Halo.

5 pairs of DMC 80 Cordonnet Special as passives. Cut 5 24" (60cm) lengths.
1 pair of DMC 80 Cordonnet Special as workers. Cut 1 72" (200cm) length.
1 pair of Twilley's Gold Dust as outside passives. Cut 1 24" (60cm) length.

Hang the glittery outside passives on T1, then hang the workers from the same pin and interlink them keeping the workers on the right. Twist the workers twice, but don't twist the glittery passive pair at all. Hang two pairs on each of pins T2 & T3, and one pair on T4. Interlink the pairs on T2 and twist each pair twice, repeat with the pairs on T3. Take the righthand pair from T3 and work a half stitch with the pair from T4, put up pin 5 and cover it with another half stitch, remove pin T4 and tension both pairs carefully. Work ground stitches (half stitch, pin, half stitch) on pin 6, 7 & 8. Now work the fan twisting the workers twice inside the glittery outer passive pair and twice at the end of every row. Twist each of the passive pairs coming out of the fan once and then complete the area of ground with the usual half stitch, pin, half stitch on pins 23-32. Repeat from pin 9 until the circle is complete. At the end use a crochet hook to bring one thread of each pair through its corresponding starting loop or pinhole, tie each pair with a reef knot & trim off the ends.

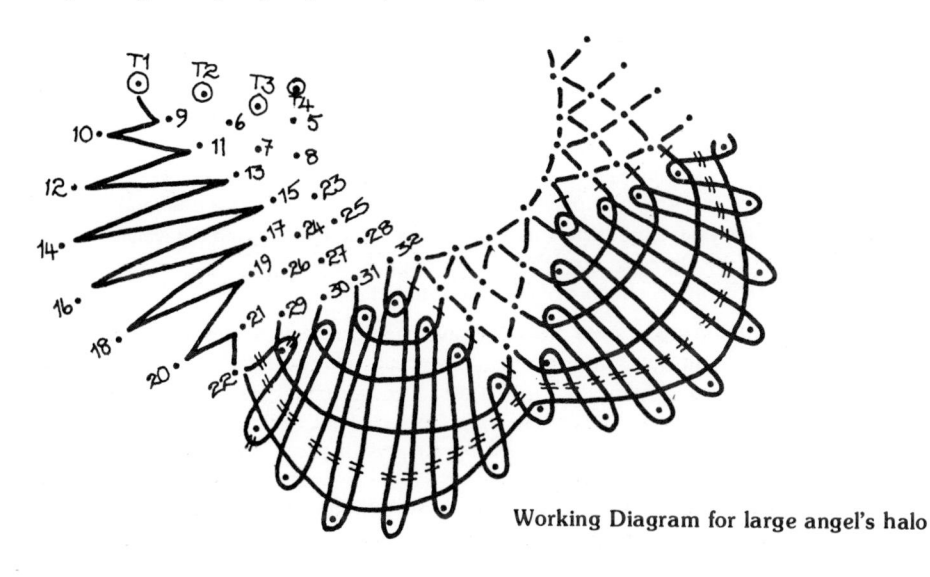

Working Diagram for large angel's halo

4 small Angels

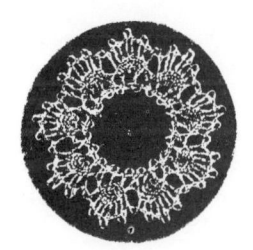

Small angel's finished halo

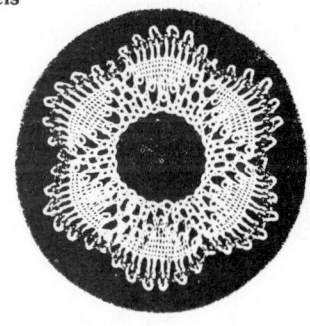

Large angel's finished halo

71

EQUIPMENT.

Bobbins. Although it is possible to economise and use substitutes for many of the other items on this equipment list I think most lace teachers would agree that there is no substitute for bobbins. Always buy the best that you can afford, inexpensive plastic bobbins or the cheapest wooden bobbin will get you started, but whichever you choose make sure that the head shape is well defined and smooth enough to allow the thread to slide easily without snagging.

Beads. English lace bobbins are usually weighted with a ring of beads at the end of the shank, and because weight is important it is essential to use glass beads for the 'spangle', plastic beads will not be satisfactory. The spangle usually consists of a single larger bead with several smaller ones on each side which you may like to arrange in diminishing size so that the smallest are situated on each side of the bobbin.

Wire. The glass beads of the spangle are traditionally threaded on brass wire which can be purchased from lace equipment suppliers.

Pillow. Lace is traditionally made on a straw pillow, but many lacemakers today buy the very inexpensive polystyrene pillows which can be padded with several layers of carpet underfelt or an old woollen blanket to prevent the surface breaking up so readily. A simple round pillow 16"-18" (40-45cm) in diameter is fine to begin with. It is possible to use a thick piece of polystyrene insulating material but it is not so easy to make lace on a completely flat surface, so try and shape the top to make a slight dome.

Cover-Cloths. Whatever shape or material your pillow the surface should always be covered with fabric which can be removed and washed when necessary. You should choose a fabric in a plain colour, most lacemakers choose dark green or blue. The fabric itself should have a smooth finish and should be pre-washed to make sure that neither colour nor loose fluff or 'lint' will be transferred to your lace thread as the bobbins are moved over it. A plain woven cotton or 'drill' fabric is best. You will need not only a cover for your pillow, but also at least two square cover cloths with which to 'dress' your pillow once the pricking is pinned in place. These will ensure that your bobbins always move over a smooth surface. One cloth should be kept to place over your pillow whenever you stop working, this will help to keep your lace clean. Dark coloured men's handkerchiefs can be used as cover cloths.

Pins. Traditionally brass pins are used for lace and these can be purchased from lace equipment suppliers. Obviously it is possible to use ordinary dressmaking pins if nothing else is available. Children need fairly sturdy pins as fine pins are easily bent.

Pattern or Pricking. There are two ways of making a pricking. Firstly you can use the more traditional way of transferring the pattern onto a piece of special pricking card. For this you will need a photocopy of the pattern, the pricking card, a cork pricking board and a pricker. Place the photocopy over the card and place both on the pricking board. Using the pricker (a needle held firmly in a wooden handle or 'chuck') make a hole wherever there is a dot. Remove the photocopy and copy the markings onto the card. It is very important to take care in both steps as your lace can only be as good as your pricking, a poor pricking can never allow you to make good lace. Many lacemakers today prefer to photocopy the pattern directly from the book onto a piece of ordinary card. If you wish you can place clear or blue matt film over the pattern to make sure that none of the marking comes off on your thread. You can then prick the pattern before you start, or you can make the holes as you go along. With children it is much more accurate to prick the pattern first. As children don't usually want to repeat the same pattern time after time the second method is probably quite acceptable.

Pinlifter. This is a very useful gadget which does precisely what its name suggests — lifts pins which have been pressed all the way down into the pillow by means of a small forked metal prong.

Crochet Hook. I use a .6mm hook for a variety of tasks such as making 'sewings' or joining together work at the finish.

Lazy Susan. Another useful little tool which can be used instead of a crochet hook. Basically it consists of a needle mounted in a wooden handle so that the eye of the needle faces outwards.

Stitch Holder. To keep the bobbins in order whilst the pillow is being moved, or when the lace is moved up the pattern, you can use a knitting stitch holder, or a piece of ribbon or tape which is threaded through the spangles of the bobbins.

Thread. Where a fine glittery metallic thread is required you can use:-
    Mez Effektgarn, fine Madeira or DMC Metalise.
Where a thicker glitter thread is required use:-
    Twilley's Gold Dust (NOT the commoner Gold Fingering which is thicker)
    Madeira in the familiar 20m flat packs.
    (When using these threads with children it is wise to tie a simple knot at the end of the cut length to prevent it unravelling as the bobbins are wound.)
    Where I have used white thread you may find the following equivalents useful:-
    36/2 BROK cotton or DMC 30 Retors d'Alsace.
    100/3 BROK cotton or DMC 50 Retors d'Alsace.

Glue. To mount many of these projects I have used glue such as Bostik, Uhu, Copydex and just plain paper gum such as Gloy. Always use glue extremely sparingly and with appropriate caution.

If you have problems obtaining any accessories for these projects write to:
C & D Springett, 21 Hillmorton Road, Rugby, Warwickshire, CV22 5DF. Tel: (0788) 544691